WHAT'S SO FUNNY
ABOUT
BEING CATHOLIC?

WHAT'S SO FUNNY ABOUT BEING CATHOLIC?

An Uproarious Collection of Blasphemous Facts, Unholy Jokes, Irreverent Folklore, and More

Karen Warner

Illustrations by Kathleen O'Malley

HarperPerennial

A Division of HarperCollinsPublishers

HarperCollins books may be purchased for educational, business, or sales promotional use. For information, please write: Special Markets Department, HarperCollins Publishers, Inc., 10 East 53rd Street, New York, NY 10022.

FIRST EDITION

Designed by George J. McKeon

Library of Congress Cataloging-in-Publication Data
What's so funny about being Catholic? : a spirited collection of unsanctioned facts and irreverent folklore / [compiled] by Karen Warner.
    p.   cm.
  ISBN 0-06-095023-4 (pbk.)
  1. Catholic wit and humor.
PN6231.C22W43   1994
282'.0207—dc20   93-39547

94 95 96 97 98 ❖/CW 10 9 8 7 6 5 4 3 2 1

This book is dedicated to my family and my longtime and newfound friends who took the time to be interviewed and share their Catholic experiences:

Marie Aranas, Sacred Heart parish, San Francisco, California

Craig Bashel, American Martyrs parish, Manhattan Beach, California

Geri M. Boelcke, Queen of Martyrs parish, Evergreen Park, Illinois

Brian Bouldrey, St. Mary Star of the Sea parish, Jackson, Michigan

Joann Boyle, St. Walter's parish, Chicago, Illinois

Richard Boyle, St. Adrian's parish, Chicago, Illinois

Jim Breheney, St. Gabriel's parish, Stamford, Connecticut

Linda Kay Bristow, Methodist, Divernon, Illinois

Peter W. Butler, Immaculate Conception parish, Elmhurst, Illinois

Tony Byrne, St. Mary's Haddington Road parish, Dublin, Ireland

William J. Callahan, St. Aidan's parish, Jersey City, New Jersey

Michele Canning, St. Ethelreda's parish, Chicago, Illinois

Michael Sountru Caulfield, St. Eugene's parish, Chicago, Illinois

Agnes Consolacion, St. Mary's Cathedral, San Francisco, California

Jay Constable, St. Gertrude's parish, Chicago, Illinois

Brian Conway, St. Mary's parish, Nutley, New Jersey

Diane Conway, Methodist, San Rafael, California

Betty Czekala, Little Flower parish, Chicago, Illinois

Bill Dolon, Our Lady of Grace parish, Penndel, Pennsylvania

John Duff, St. Peter's parish, Troy, New York

Patricia Duff, Protestant, Denver, Colorado

Will Dunne, St. Mary's parish, Chicago, Illinois

Craig Farinelli, Saint Michael's parish, Penn Yan, New York

Dawn Fischer, St. Walter's parish, Chicago, Illinois

Alberta J. Fox, St. Patricia's parish, Hickory Hills, Illinois

Kathy Fox, St. Leo's parish, Chicago, Illinois

Marcella Friel, St. Colman's parish, Ardmore, Pennsylvania

John Gallagher, St. Matthew's parish, Cranston, Rhode Island

Gracemarie Good, Our Lady of the Ridge parish, Chicago Ridge, Illinois

Kevin C. Good, Our Lady of the Ridge parish, Chicago Ridge, Illinois

Marie A. Good, Our Lady of the Ridge parish, Chicago Ridge, Illinois

Margaret Komet Hensley, Saints Simon and Jude's parish, Brooklyn, New York

Daniel Hernandez, Holy Family's parish, San Antonio, Texas

Cheryl K. Hylton, Unitarian, Chicago, Illinois

Michael Iapoce, St. Mary's parish, Long Island City, Queens, New York

Linda Johnson, Blessed Sacrament parish, Waterbury, Connecticut

Madelyn P. Johnson, Our Lady of the Ridge parish, Chicago Ridge, Illinois

Rick Kelleher, Sacred Heart parish, East Grand Forks, Minnesota

Rory (Rosemary) Keller, St. William's parish, Cincinnati, Ohio

Tom Kole, St. Leo's parish, Chicago, Illinois

Christine Kowal, Our Lady of Lourdes parish, Decatur, Illinois

Jack Kowal, St. Leo's parish, Chicago, Illinois

Peter Kowal, St. Leo's parish, Chicago, Illinois

Shirley Kowal, St. Leo's parish, Chicago, Illinois

Timothy Patrick McCarthy, St. Joseph's parish, Long Island City, New York City, New York

Kathy McGilvery, St. Brendan's parish, San Francisco, California

Becky McGovern, Holy Family parish, Peoria, Illinois

Joseph McInerney, St. Joseph's parish, Limerick, Ireland

Coleen Martin, Christ the King parish, Chicago, Illinois

Pat Melloni, Queen of Martyr's parish, Evergreen Park, Illinois

C. Kimberly Regan, Holy Spirit's parish, Stamford, Connecticut

Mary Regan, no religious affiliation, Livermore, California

Peggy Regnier, St. Leo's parish, Chicago, Illinois

Robert Regnier, St. John the Baptist's parish, Chicago, Illinois

Dave Roberts, St. Joseph's parish, Wilmette, Illinois

Mitchel A. Robuck, St. John Cancius parish, East Chicago, Indiana

Joan Each Rowan, St. Bride's parish, Chicago, Illinois

Annette Sandoval, Our Lady of the Pillar parish, Santa Ana, California

Susan Santos, St. Genevieve's parish, Van Nuys, California

Matt Schleder, St. Bernadette's parish, Evergreen Park, Illinois

Dan Shaughnessy, Sacred Heart parish, Groton, Massachusetts

Bridget Dubriwny Sielaff, St. Joan of Arc's parish, St. Clair Shores, Michigan

Jill Stanley, St. Leo's parish, Chicago, Illinois

Sally Starr, St. Louis of France's parish, Chicago, Illinois

Donna Swift, St. Etheldreda's parish, Chicago, Illinois

John Sylvester, Queen of Martyrs parish, Evergreen Park, Illinois

Inez H. Templeton, Methodist, Rock Mount, North Carolina

Jan Wahl, movie critic, KRON-TV, San Francisco, California

Tom Watkins, Holy Angels' parish, Arcadia, California

Joe Weatherby, Our Lady of Mercy parish, Sarnia, Ontario, Canada

Rosemary D. Wesela, Saints Peter and Paul parish, Milwaukee, Wisconsin

Patricia Kowal West, St. Leo's parish, Chicago, Illinois

Judith A. Winters, Presbyterian, Freeport, Illinois

Jonathan Yorba, St. Martha's parish, La Puente, California

Ed Zotti, St. Catherine of Siena parish, Oak Park, Illinois

CONTENTS

ACKNOWLEDGMENTS

A heartfelt thank you to the following people:

The elusive Cecil Adams and his hardworking assistant Ed Zotti for granting me an interview and permission to reprint articles from *The Straight Dope*.

Brian Bouldrey and Will Dunne for writing very funny essays and stories.

Patti Breitman, my literary agent extraordinaire.

John Callahan, wild funnyman, for allowing me to reprint his cartoons.

Myron Cope, Dan "Rudy" Reuttiger, and Roger Staubach for taking the time from their busy schedules to allow me to interview them.

Eamon Dolan, who is not only a terrific editor but an expert spotter of Catholic trivia.

Albert Fox for her help in creating the Legion of Decency Crossword Puzzle.

Beth Hansen-Shaw, the talented reference librarian at Governors State University, University Park, Illinois.

The very talented Tom Lehrer for granting me permission to reprint the words and music to the "Vatican Rag."

Kathy O'Malley, my wonderful illustrator.

Nancy Sandleback, assistant archivist for the Archdiocese of Chicago.

Karen Snelson and Aimee MacDonald and all the other kind folks at Archie McPhee's.

Anne Tracy and all the very helpful folks at the Special Collections at the Michigan State University, East Lansing, Michigan.

The staff at the University of San Francisco, especially Eric Ewen, Ivan Hudson, and Dean David Oyler, for their cheerful and conscientious assistance.

INTRODUCTION

As Catholics we are defined not just by our religious beliefs but by almost every aspect of our daily lives. Where we go to school—Holy Martyrs of the Bleeding Heart. What we wear—plaid jumpers and corduroy pants. Who we marry— each other. What we eat—"Hold the pepperoni on the pizza; it's Good Friday!" What we think—no impure thoughts. What we do for fun—play Bingo. Our Catholicness spills over into every part of our lives. My Methodist friend, Diane Conway, said it best: "Catholics have more 'stuff' than other religions." We do! Catholics have a special language with exotic words like *genuflect, annunciation,* and *extreme unction.* We even have a whole assortment of religious "props": statues, holy cards, and votive candles. It is all that "stuff" that makes Catholics . . . Catholics.

With tongue in cheek, this book examines the "stuff" of our daily Catholic lives. *What's So Funny About Being Catholic?* is a collection of jokes, news reports, personal interviews, sports trivia, and religious gift items that are often ridiculous, frequently silly, and sometimes just downright funny.

A WORD OF THANKS

This book contains hundreds of anecdotes collected from interviews with Catholics and non-Catholics from around the country. I have identified each of the interviewees by name, parish, and hometown.

A DISCLAIMER

In the interest of fair play and to protect their anonymity, I have changed the names for all the priests, nuns, brothers, and laypeople mentioned in the personal anecdotes and stories. I have not changed the names of people whose lives are of historical significance or are a matter of public record as described in books, reference material and newspapers, magazines, or tabloid articles.

1

GRISLY FACT AND FOLKLORE
FROM THE FAITHFUL

After we put away our Baltimore Catechism books, Sister Victoria Cecilia would fill our young minds with romantic tales of the lives of saints. Sister would describe in graphic detail how the saints had been skinned alive, impaled on swords, stretched on racks, and disemboweled. Naturally, these saintly examples left an indelible impression and gave rise to our own collection of grisly fact and folklore.

Brother Claw

I went to school in the barrio in Santa Ana. We were taught by a Franciscan order and the janitors were Franciscan brothers too. They were responsible for cleaning the school. The brothers had taken a vow of silence. All these silent men would be scrubbing the floors and washing the windows.

There was one brother—I don't remember his name but all the kids called him "The Claw." In this order when a member of your family died you had to cut off a part of your finger to show your grief. I'm not sure if this was a Mexican custom or a custom from the religious order. Anyway, poor Claw, he was the youngest member of a very large family. When we met him he was a very old man and only had a thumb and his index finger on either hand. But he did manage to mop and sweep with no problem. All of us wondered, because of his vow of silence, if when they cut off his finger he said "ouch."

—*Annette Sandoval, Our Lady of the Pillar parish, Santa Ana, California*

My Favorite Saint

When I was about eleven years old I would go on retreats. The retreats were like campouts with lectures. We would go off and hang out near the grottos and smoke cigarettes and be punks. One grotto had a statue of Saint Sebastian. Saint Sebastian was the martyr who had been shot with thousands of arrows. This was not your ordinary statue of Saint Sebastian—it was anatomically correct. He was bleeding from every pore. It was very cool.

—*Ed Zotti, St. Catherine of Siena's parish, Oak Park, Illinois*

The Nun with the Wooden Leg

Sister Murial liked the boys better than the girls. She used to shoot craps in the parking lot against the car bumpers with the boys. The thing I remember most about her was she had a limp. The story circulated among the kids that she was part Indian and had done something to offend her tribe so the Indians cut off her leg and replaced it with a wooden leg. I never looked under her habit so I don't know if she really had a fake leg. —*Dawn Fischer, St. Walter's parish, Chicago, Illinois*

What's Cooking?

The Feast of the Holy Innocents is the day the infants of Bethlehem were murdered by Herod because he believed the newborn Christ to be a rival king. We honor the Holy Innocents as the first martyrs.

In joy, at least have a dessert in their name. German cooks created a Bavarian cream with either a strawberry or cherry sauce to symbolize the blood that Herod spilled. They felt that blancmange would be suitable for little children and grownups after too much Christmas feasting.

—*From* Cooking for Christ *by Florence S. Berger*

Scaring the Bejeepers Out of Us

The old nuns used to try and scare the bejeepers out of us. One of them told us a story of a man who had been buried and for some reason was dug up again. He was alive when he was buried and while he was in the coffin he had eaten his fingers and hair.

—*Shirley Kowal, St. Margaret's parish, Chicago, Illinois*

The Head on the Railroad Track

If you made nine First Friday masses in a row you were given an ironclad guarantee that you would not die with a mortal sin on your soul. By way of illustration, the nun told us about a boy playing on the railroad tracks who was hit by a train and decapitated. His body was lying on one side of the tracks and his head on the other. Shocked onlookers rushed up and the head of the boy opened its eyes and said, "Get me a priest!" Because at some point in his short life, the child had made the nine First Fridays and God would not let him die with sin on his soul. They got a priest and the priest heard his confession and gave the head extreme unction. I don't think he gave the last rites to the body, just the head.

—*William J. Callahan, St. Aidan's parish, Jersey City, New Jersey*

Just Like Jesus

We had this wild grass growing near the school—it was thick and very sharp. The older kids would say to the first-graders, "Hold still." They'd whip it back and forth and slice our foreheads. They'd say, "It's like Jesus, you're bleeding."

—*Brian Conway, St. Mary's parish, Nutley, New Jersey*

The Priest with Stumps for Hands

Saint Isaac Jogues (1607–1646) was the only priest the church permitted to hold the Holy Eucharist with mutilated hands. Saint Jogues was a missionary to the Huron Indians but was caught and held captive by the Mohawks. The Mohawk Indian women slowly chewed off his fingers until they were just stumps. When he got back to France he petitioned Pope Urban VIII to get a pardon to hold the host.

—*Betty Czekala, Little Flower parish, Chicago, Illinois*

2

THE TRUTH ABOUT PAROCHIAL SCHOOL

Now they can be told! The shocking scandals from the classrooms of parochial schools: collecting money for pagan babies, impersonating the Virgin Mary, cigarette-smoking nuns, and much, much more.

Two Unofficial (But Universal) Parochial School Songs

Sung to the tune of "Heigh-Ho"
Heigh-ho, heigh-ho
It's off to school we go
With razor blades and hand grenades
Heigh-ho, heigh-ho

Heigh-ho, heigh-ho
It's off to school we go
With tommy guns to shoot the nuns
Heigh-ho, heigh-ho

Sung to the Tune of "When the Caissons Go Rolling Along"
We are brave, we are bold, and there's whiskey to be sold
In the cellars of St. Coleman's School
Run, run, run, I think I hear a nun
Grab all the whiskey and run
If a nun should appear say, "Sister, have a beer!"
In the cellars of St. Coleman's School
  —Marcella Friel, St. Coleman's parish, Ardmore, Pennsylvania

I Am the Immaculate Conception

In the third grade I had long blond hair that I wore in braids, a very angelic look. I was one of the "good" kids in my class. I always did what Sister Rose said, so of course I was one of her favorites. She liked me so much that she gave me my first and only chance at a starring role in a theatrical performance. She selected me, from all the other girls in her third-grade class, to be the Immaculate Conception. Since I was only eight years old, I wasn't sure who or what the Immaculate Conception was.

My mom made a snow-white gown and Sister had a blue mantle for me to wear as part of my costume. I had to memorize a speech that started out with the words, "I am the Immaculate Conception" . . . I don't remember the rest. Sister Rose got me all decked out in my Virgin Mary outfit with my hair flowing down my back. She paraded me around from classroom to classroom re-creating the vision of Our Blessed Mother. I would stand on top of a tiny stool and five or six first-grade students (dressed in their school uniforms) would kneel at my feet with their hands folded and pointed toward heaven. I would clear my throat and extend my arms with open hands and my fingers separated (Sister Rose was very clear that I was to keep hands open and fingers separated). After getting in position, I would give my speech. Then I would step down and pick up the tiny stool and the "Traveling Immaculate Conception Show" would move on to the next classroom.

My brief stint as the Blessed Virgin was a legacy I felt I never lived down for the rest of my days at St. Etheldreda's grade school. The boys branded me a nerd. It haunted me even into the eighth grade. Out of nowhere one of the guys teased me by saying, "Oh, Michele, don't talk to her, she thinks she's the Virgin Mary."

I couldn't wait to graduate and leave the Immaculate Conception behind.

—*Michele Canning, St. Etheldreda's parish, Chicago, Illinois*

Why did the cannibal eat the missionary?
He wanted a taste of religion.

Ransoming Pagan Babies

In fourth and fifth grades pagan babies were a big thing. After that we discovered the opposite sex and we weren't interested anymore. The nuns would collect money to "ransom"—that was the word they used—to ransom pagan babies. I don't remember how much it cost, but ten dollars rings a bell. We had competitions of the boys against the girls to see who could save the most pagans. The girls consistently ransomed more pagan babies than the boys. I think the boys just didn't care as much. When your team ransomed a pagan you got to name the baby. The girls always named them Mary or Teresa and the boys would pick Michael or William. It's a funny thing but we never called the babies anything creative like Francis Xavier or Ignatius Loyola.

—*Bill Dolon, Our Lady of Grace parish, Penndel, Pennsylvania*

Sister said, "How many of you children want to go to heaven?"

"I can't, Sister," said Alice. "I have to go right home after school."

He Sure Dressed Like a Commie

When I was in the fourth grade there were persecutions going on in Mexico. Sister Mary Joseph used to tell us that maybe one day we would be called on to proclaim our faith and give up our life. Because the communists were everywhere, we would become martyrs for Christ. One spring day, Sister was looking out the window and saw a man with a red jacket and a red duffle bag. The man was going door to door handing out leaflets. Sister Mary Joseph was convinced the man was a communist. Sister told Rich O'Connor and I to go out and bring back a leaflet from the hated communist infiltrator. He was passing out advertisements from Goldblatt's Department Store.

—*Bob Regnier, St. John the Baptist parish, Chicago, Illinois*

What's Vat 69?
The pope's phone number.

The Picket Line

There was a drugstore down the block from Saint Matthew's. We used to go there after school to buy candy and hang out. The guy who owned the shop sold magazines—the usual stuff—*Look*, *Life*, and *Time*. He also had some girlie magazines. The nuns were outraged. They sent all the students to picket in front of his store in protest. Here we were—a bunch of seven-year-old kids protesting against girlie magazines. The poor guy. He ended up moving the magazines off the rack.

—*John Gallagher, St. Matthew's parish, Cranston, Rhode Island*

"Sister, last night I had sex," announced Billy in class one day.

"Billy," asked the amazed sister, "do you know what sex is?"

"Everyone knows, it's the number after five."

Passing Time While Sister Snoozed

We had this really old nun, Sister Lloyd, who used to fall asleep during class. So whenever Sister nodded off, Carole, who was the biggest girl in class—she was wearing a bra in second grade—would get up and write "color" on the blackboard. Everyone would take out their coloring book and color until Sister Lloyd woke up.

—*Madelyn Johnson, Our Lady of the Ridge parish, Chicago Ridge, Illinois*

What's Jesus's phone number?
Et Cum Spiritus Tuo.

Why I Became a Hairdresser

I am a hairdresser and have always been obsessed with hair. I went to Catholic school for the first two years of my education. During those two years I was preoccupied with the notion that I might catch a glimpse of the nuns' hair. Sister would be in the front of the room writing on the blackboard. If she moved a certain way, I could see a wisp of hair. It drove me crazy.

—*Craig Farinelli, Saint Michael's parish, Penn Yan, New York*

Two Catholic boys walked by an Episcopalian minister. One of the boys spotted his collar and said, "Good morning, Father."

The other boy said, "He's no father, you idiot. He's married and has six kids."

Get Your Whats-it Out of the Whose-it?

If anyone had their feet in the aisle between rows of desks, Sister would yell, "Get your gun-boats out of the issel." She pronounced aisle "issel."

—*Kathy Fox, St. Leo's parish, Chicago, Illinois*

Frankenstein and the pope arrive at the Pearly Gates at the same time. Saint Peter says, "We're all filled up right now. I only have room for one more. Go ahead in, Frankenstein."

The pope can't believe it. He says, "Why did you let that monster in heaven and not me, the Holy Father?"

Saint Peter says, "To be honest with you, Your Holiness, he's scared the hell out of more people than you have."

Sister B.J.

In sixth grade we had Sister Basil John. We called her Big John or B.J. She must have been almost six feet tall and weighed two hundred pounds. She looked like a linebacker on the Chicago Bears.

Three of us were supposed to clean up the Little League field during the forty-five-minute recess. Sister told us to pick up papers and patrol the area. After about twenty minutes, I just sat down on the bleachers and let the other two guys do all the work. Sister B.J. had been spying on me through the window with a pair of binoculars. When I got back into class she called me into the hallway. She was yelling at me and I don't know why, but it struck me as funny, and I started laughing. B.J. hauled off and hit me in the stomach as hard as she could. It didn't hurt and I started laughing again. She gave up and sent me to the principal's office and I got put on detention that Saturday. The fact that I could see the humor in the situation made me feel like I had won a victory over Sister B.J.

—*Craig Bashel, American Martyrs parish, Manhattan Beach, California*

When he entered the cannibal village the missionary met with the head of the tribe and let the chief know that he was a strict vegetarian.

The chief said, "No problem, Father. We're all strict human-itarians."

Well, What Color Are They?

We had an exchange nun from India teaching at our grade school. She was very frustrated because we didn't really take any interest in her background. One day she said, "Why don't you ever ask me questions about my country? Don't you want to know about where I come from?" So I raised my hand and said, "Sister, what color are your license plates?"

—*Annette Sandoval, Our Lady of the Pillar parish, Santa Ana, California*

Sister Mary Catherine asked her first-grade class, "Name two things that are necessary for a baptism."

Roger stood up and said, "I know, Sister. Water and a baby."

Getting Your Priorities Straight

All the boys were considered potential priests. The best a girl could aspire to was to become a nun. In the fourth grade the priests would come around to each classroom and ask, "How many boys are going to become priests?" "How many girls are going to be nuns?" All the boys and girls would raise their hands. It was nothing more than peer pressure. The arch-diocese would try to get the boys into the seminary right after grammar school. They wanted to get us before we had a high school experience and went through the rest of our puberty. There were a couple of us who the monsignor considered good candidates for the priesthood.

One afternoon, waiting in his chambers in his red robes, the monsignor said to my best friend and I, "Have you fellows decided if you are going to the seminary?" It was a very intimidating atmosphere. I told him that it wasn't for me even though I was actually very spiritual. I wasn't interested in the priesthood because I was more interested in girls.

—*Anonymous, St. Gabriel's parish, San Francisco, California*

Sister Catherine asked her second-grade class, "Who can tell me the story of Easter?"

"I can, Sister," said Cathy. "They nailed Jesus to the cross, then they buried Him in the cave and rolled the big rock in front of it."

"Then what happened?" asked Sister.

"Then Jesus was alive and He came out of the tomb and saw His shadow, so there were six more weeks of winter."

Wait Till Joe Camel Hears About This

In the third grade the nun sent me to the teachers' lounge to get something. I opened the door and all these nuns were sitting around smoking cigarettes. I ran out of the room and started to cry. Sister Aquinas followed me and said, "Don't worry, nuns are human too."

—*Coleen Martin, Christ the King parish, Chicago, Illinois*

3

A COLLECTION OF SACRILEGIOUS PAROCHIAL SCHOOL JOKES

It is a tradition that rowdy parochial school kids everywhere tell raunchy, tasteless, and sacrilegious jokes the minute the sisters are out of earshot.

Mary and Joseph are in the stable waiting for the baby to be born. Joseph is gathering straw to put in the manger when he stubs his toe. "Jesus Christ," he yells.

Mary looks up and says, "That's a good name!"

Saint Peter is working at the Pearly Gates when the lunch whistle blows. He grabs his lunchbox but his replacement doesn't show up to relieve him. Saint Peter gets on the phone and calls Jesus and asks Him if He could fill in at the Pearly Gates for an hour. Jesus agrees and He is standing at the *entrance to heaven with a clipboard when an old man appears.*

Jesus says to the old man, "What's your name?"

"Well," says the gray-haired man, "in English it would be Joseph."

"What did you do for a living?" asks Christ.

"I was a humble working man, a carpenter."

Jesus becomes curious and asks, "Did you have any children?"

"Just one, a son," answers the old man.

Jesus becomes very excited and asks, "Was there anything out of the ordinary about your son's birth?"

"Let's just say, " says the man, "he wasn't born in the usual way."

Jesus is so happy he can barely contain Himself. He asks, "When was the last time you saw your son?"

"It's been more years than I can remember."

Jesus throws the clipboard in the air and runs to embrace the old man, crying, "Daddy!"

"Pinocchio?"

What were Jesus's last words on the cross?
"This is a hell of a way to spend Easter vacation!"

A Roman soldier is whipping Jesus as He carries His cross up the hill. The Roman looks at the sundial strapped to his wrist and realizes that it is time for his fifteen-minute break. The soldier and Christ sit down on the side of the road. First the solider lights up a cigarette and then Jesus pulls a pack out of His robe.

The soldier says, "Oh, I see you smoke Raleighs."

"Of course," says Jesus. "How do you think I got this cross?"

Why can't Jesus eat M&M's?
They fall through the holes in His hands.

Christ has been hanging on the cross for hours. In a barely audible voice He calls out, "Mary . . . Mary . . . Mary . . . "

"Yes, my son," says Mary, "what are you trying to tell me?"

Jesus whispers, "Mary . . . Mary . . . Mary . . . "

"I'm right here," answers the Virgin Mother. "I can hear you, what is it?"

Using all His strength, Jesus lifts His bloodied head and looks over the horizon. "Mary . . . Mary . . . Mary . . . "

Fighting back the tears, she says, "Yes, my Lord."

"Mary . . . Mary . . . I can see our house from here."

What did the Roman gladiator say to Jesus while he was nailing Him to the cross?

"Could you cross your legs? I've only got three spikes."

Jesus grew furious when he spotted a group of people throwing stones at a woman. Running to save the woman, he yelled, "Let he who is without sin cast the first stone."

Just then a rock came flying from the crowd.

Staring into the mob, Jesus swore, "Damn it, is that you again, Mother?"

Did you hear about that new punk rock group? Pontius Pilot and the Nailers.

Why didn't Jesus go to college?

He got nailed on the boards.

Anyone caught reading or repeating these jokes will be smacked on the knuckles with a ruler by Sister Mary Disciplino. Remember Sister's guidelines: Thinking about these jokes is a venial sin, laughing at these jokes is a mortal sin, and repeating these jokes is grounds for excommunication.

4

ARE YOU PREPARED TO DIE FOR YOUR FAITH?

Corporal and Other Forms of Punishment

Sister Felicity hit Jimmy Nolan in the head with her rosary beads and Sister Damien made us all line up to give us group punishment with her yardstick. The good nuns would never have had to resort to such extremes unless we deserved it. Or did we?

The first day of algebra class Sister asked the class, "What is the answer to problem number one? Bill, do you know?"

"It's goddamn X squared."

Sister took Billy by the ear and dragged him out of his seat, whacked him with her ruler, and locked him in the cloakroom.

"James, what is the answer to problem number one?"

"The answer is X squared, goddamn it!"

Outraged, Sister took Jimmy by the collar and pulled him to the front of the classroom. She made him stand in a wastepaper basket facing the corner.

"*Now then, Frank, what is the correct answer to problem number one?*"

"*Well Sister, you can bet your rosary beads it's not goddamn X squared.*"

Would That Be a Coffee Table or a Sectional Sofa?

Sister Dympna pointed to me one day because I was talking to the kid next to me. Sister said, "You down there with the furniture on your face." The "furniture on your face" referred to my glasses. She came flying down the aisle with her veil streaming behind her. Wham. My furniture went flying.

—*Betty Czekala, Little Flower parish, Chicago, Illinois*

The Kid's Got Stick-to-It-iveness

The monsignor was giving out report cards and he caught Jack Callaghan chewing gum. Jack had to put the gum on the tip of his nose and stand with the tip of his nose connected to the blackboard for an hour or so.

—*Kathy McGilvery, St. Brendan's parish, San Francisco, California*

An Alternative to the Palmer Method

The punishment meted out in our class was to be routinely hit on the forehead with a pair of scissors. Sister would sneak up on us when we were practicing our penmanship. As a result, I have really good handwriting.

—*Mitchel A. Robuck, St. John Cancius' parish, East Chicago, Indiana*

You Get More Than Lunch in This Cafeteria

When I was in the sixth grade, during a basketball game three of my friends snuck into the bathroom. The opposing girls' basketball team had to keep their bags in the bathroom because they didn't have lockers. We took all the tampons from the dispenser and put them all over the opposing team's bags. We thought this was a terribly funny thing to do. Of course, we got caught. That was on Friday. The following

Monday we were punished. During lunch the nun called our names: "Christine Kowal, Terry Ward, and Lonnie Bates." Sister asked us if we were guilty and of course we admitted it. Right there in the cafeteria in front of everyone we had to bend over and get paddled.

—*Christine Kowal, Our Lady of Lourdes parish, Decatur, Illinois*

Ready, Aim, Fire

We had one priest who was an absolute expert at hitting you with his chalk. He never had to send anyone to jug or use the vice-principal to discipline us. He just threw chalk. He was uncanny. He'd be writing on the blackboard and he could sense which guy was screwing up. All of a sudden he'd turn and fire. He'd always hit the exact guy who was screwing up. We secretly admired his marksmanship.

—*Anonymous, St. Ignatius parish, San Francisco, California*

A Perfect Record

Brother Mark, my history teacher, did not let anyone complete his class without getting smacked at least once. If you transgressed you were brought up to the front of the room, sometimes in groups of two or three, and he'd say, "Don't move, gentlemen." He'd slap you across the face. Occasionally he'd slap you on both sides of your face, depending on the severity of your transgression. Even Albert, aka "The Saint," was called up at the end of the year to be slapped, just so Brother Mark would have a perfect record.

—*John Duff, St. Peter's parish, Troy, New York*

I Prefer Mustard

One of the rowdy boys, Bill Maloney, threw his hot dog on the ground. As a punishment, Sister made him put soap on his hot dog and eat it.

—*Susan Santos, St. Genevieve's parish, Van Nuys, California*

A Pointed Punishment

Sister Ann Bridget had a whistle and a thin wooden pointer. When she blew the whistle you were supposed to freeze (like you would when you were playing statue maker) and she'd say, "Stop talking" or "Don't do that." Occasionally she'd yank someone out of line and give him a slap on the hand with her wooden pointer.

—*Marie Aranas, Sacred Heart parish, San Francisco, California*

The Hunker Walk

The Christian Brothers of Ireland made us walk on our hunkers around the school yard.

—*Joseph McInerney, St. Joseph's parish, Limerick, Ireland*

George, one of the troublemakers in class, was listening to Brother O'Hara talk about the wonders of God's miracles. "Hey Father," said George, "what is a miracle, anyway?"

Brother O'Hara said, "The best way to show you is to demonstrate. Please, George, bend over." George bent over and Brother gave him a tremendous kick right between the legs. Howling in pain, George dropped to his knees. Brother O'Hara said, "George, did you feel that?"

"Of course I did," whimpered George.

"If you hadn't," said Brother O'Hara, "that would have been a miracle."

Another Use for *Webster's* Unabridged

Sister Andrew Thomas told troublemaker Harry to come to the front of the class. She had this giant unabridged dictionary. Sister told Harry to bend over. She held the dictionary like a baseball bat; he put his hands to cover his butt. Smack. Harry went flying.

—*Coleen Martin, Our Lady of Lourdes parish, Decatur, Illinois*

Fastest Way to Search a Student

Sister Victoria caught one of the boys in the class stealing. She took him by the ankles, lifted him up in the air, and shook him until everything fell out of his pockets.

—*Bridget Sielaff, St. Joan of Arc's parish, St. Clare Shores, Michigan*

The Stations of the Cross Crawl

Every Friday during Lent our class had to do mass and stations of the cross. At communion I would line up with about 150 other kids. The procedure was you would get in line and kneel down while you were waiting and stand up when the line moved and then kneel down again. I was a smartass and thought it was ridiculous to stand up, kneel down, stand up, kneel down, so I crawled on my hands and knees all the way up there. A nun caught me and I was called into the principal's office. I spent a lot of time in the principal's office.

—*Craig Bashel, American Martyrs parish, Manhattan Beach, California*

The High Cost of Therapy

I was in the fourth or fifth grade and I was just terrible in arithmetic. The most important thing in the world to me was pleasing the nuns—being a "good girl." But I just couldn't get math at all. I knew I'd get caught if I cheated and looked on someone else's paper. I paid very close attention when the nun put the answer book away in the bottom drawer. I looked longingly at that drawer and thought, "I don't have a choice. I have to take the answer book because I have to be right." After school, I waited until no one was around. Slowly, I opened the drawer and reached in for the book. A long black arm appeared on my shoulder. "Margaret, I can't believe it's you! How could you?"

I let the nuns down. I can't tell you how much money that incident has cost me in therapy.

—*Margaret Komet Hensley, Saints Simon and Jude parish,*
Brooklyn, New York

Drawing Dirty Pictures

I was always a little brown nose in grammar school. One time I was hanging around with a group of girls in third grade and we would draw dirty pictures. I never really saw body parts but I drew tits and a penis on control paper and I labeled the parts. I passed the paper to Kim, one of my friends in the classroom. Kim was supposed to pass it to Clare but she finked on me and told the nun. The nun squinted her eyes and stared at me but didn't say anything, so I thought, "Maybe this isn't that bad." At three o'clock the nun said, "The whole class is dismissed except Kathy McGilvery." I had to sit there while she walked the class down the corridor. I was in big, big trouble. I had to go sit with the nun in the convent while she called my mother. My mother had to come to the convent and she was crying. I was suspended, but just over the weekend, so nobody really knew. My father always went out on Friday nights, so my mother had to have one of her friends come over and stay with her because she was so upset.

The next day my mother dragged me out of bed and I had to write out and number "I have done a terrible thing" a thousand times on control paper. This for my mother! She learned good punishments from the nuns and used them on me. Later that day she made me go to confession to confess this terrible sin. I went to the easy priest, Father McInnis. I said, "I disrespected my parents twice. I told a lie twice." I tried to slip in the terrible sin by saying, "I disobeyed the sixth commandment once." Father said, "What exactly did you do?" He made me tell him what I did. I thought if my mother makes me write "I did a terrible thing" a thousand times, he's going to give me eight million Hail Mary's. He only gave me four, though.

—*Kathy McGilvery, St. Brendan's parish, San Francisco, California*

Now Am I Short Enough for You?

I was in the eighth grade in Saint Joseph's in Astoria, Queens. Sister made me kneel on the floor (because I was so tall), then she slapped me. I was punished for filling my water pistol with holy water.

—*Timothy Patrick McCarthy, St. Joseph's, Long Island City,
Queens, New York*

A Benefit of Corporal Punishment

Donald Sanchez once had his head banged against the wall by one of the Christian brothers. After getting hit, Sanchez went on to score 700 on the math portion of his SATs. And they say corporal punishment has no value!

—*Michael Iapoce, St. Mary's parish, Long Island City,
Queens, New York*

Instruments of Torture

The following is a selected guide to the instruments of torture that were used on errant students:

GET THE HOOK

Once Sister Alphonsus picked up the Boswell twins by the front of their shirts and hung them on the hooks in the cloak room by their belts.

—*Dawn Fischer, St. Walter's parish, Chicago, Illinois*

JUST THE RIGHT NOTE

A musical form of punishment was to be hit on the head with one of two types of pitch pipes: the harmonica and the round pipe. The rounded one didn't leave marks.

HOT LICKS

Mother Superior would take a jar of red pepper out of her habit and sprinkle some in the student's outstretched hand. The offending party had to lick the pepper off his hand.

NUN RUBS OUT STUDENTS

If cheating students wrote test answers on their hands, Sister used to rub them off with sandpaper.

DOUBLE TROUBLE

The triple-edge ruler on your fingers and knuckles on the top of the skull.

CLEANLINESS IS NEXT TO GODLINESS

If you had your legs in the aisle, if you didn't do your homework, or if you were caught talking the nuns would wash your mouth out with a bar of soap.

THE GAG RULE

The nun tied a rag around the mouths of talkative students.

IT'S A SMALL WORLD?

Sister would hit the wayward boys over the head with a geography book.

WHAT A WASTE

Disruptive students were made to stand in a wastepaper basket facing the chalkboard.

THAT'S WHERE THOSE PADDLES COME FROM

In woodshop class the boys made wooden paddles about 18 inches long that the sisters would use to mete out punishments. The students had to make their own instruments of torture.

5

THE SOLDIERS OF CHRIST FIGHT BACK

Undaunted by the punishments the good sisters and brothers wrought upon the wicked, the soldiers of Christ always managed to find a way to fight back.

Disarming the Enemy

The principal of our school had a wooden paddle about a foot long with holes in it. One day when she was doing lunchroom duty a group of us went into her office and took it.

—*Becky McGovern, Holy Family parish, Peoria, Illinois*

I Can't Hear You

Sister Felix wore a hearing aid. One day all the girls in the classroom agreed that when she did roll call we would lip-sync our names. She started roll call: Marcella Friel (I mouthed my name) . . . , Mary Alice Fabian (Mary Alice whispered her name). Sister said, "Oh, oh dear." She played with her hearing aid and turned it up. She continued calling the names. The next girl yelled, "HERE!"

—*Marcella Friel, St. Coleman's parish, Ardmore, Pennsylvania*

Sister was teaching her freshman students the finer points of etiquette. She said, "If a crisis should occur you must always count to twenty before you speak up."

Cathy raised her hand. "Eighteen, nineteen, twenty. . . . Sister, the cloakroom is on fire."

It's Not Exactly Perrier

Sister Ethelbert always kept an ice cold glass of water on her desk to sip while she taught. She'd send one of her students to get her a fresh glass of water. It was fresh all right! Fresh from the toilet tank.

—*Betty Czekala, Little Flower parish, Chicago, Illinois*

Sister caught Billy taking change out of the mission collection box. "Billy, don't you know you are breaking the seventh commandment. That is stealing!" said Sister.

"It's not really stealing, Sister," said Billy. "It's just that I have a talent for finding things. I just find them sometimes before they are lost."

No Money for the Missions

Brother Bonaventure, my religion teacher, was getting to be a little senile. If you contributed to the missions he would let you leave the class before the nongivers. Brother Bonaventure always collected the money in his open hands. We had it all worked out. The first couple of guys would load him up with pennies. Then the rest of us would just hit his hand like we were contributing something. We got out of class early without it costing us anything.

—*Peter Kowal, St. Leo's parish, Chicago, Illinois*

First-grader Susie raises her hand and asks Sister Mary Magdalene, "Sister, where did I come from?"

Sister blushes and says, "Susie, God sent you from heaven."

Susie says, "But, Sister, where did my mom and dad come from?"

Sister stammers and says, "God sent your parents from heaven."

Susie says, "And grandma and grandpa ... where did they come from?"

"God sent them from heaven."

"You mean to tell me that nobody in my family has had sex in seventy-five years?"

The Switch-a-Roo

The Jesuit scholastics were teachers. It was part of their education—they had to spend three years teaching. Many of them were not prepared for the experience. They had no real instruction on how to teach or how to discipline the students. We were their guinea pigs. These very spiritual young men who had been leading a semimonastic life were thrown in with a bunch of sixteen-year-old ruffians. It became a war of the wills. All the guys knew if we had a rookie; we could smell it when they walked in.

We had one scholastic, Mr. Rielly, who was a tremendous intellectual but his head was in the clouds. At our school the students would stay in the same classroom all day. The teachers would come to us to teach. We had Mr. Rielly twice in one day: in the morning for Latin, and Greek was the last class of the day. Before he came in to teach us Greek we switched the class around so everything was facing the wrong direction. Mr. Rielly came in and paused. He saw his desk in the back of the room (which was now the front of the room) and just walked up to it and started teaching like nothing was wrong. We were just falling on the floor with laughter. He began his lecture. He turned around to write on the blackboard and there was a blank wall. It never registered with him what was going on. He said, "What is it about this classroom today?"

—*Anonymous, St. Ignatius parish, San Francisco, California*

After catechism Sister asked her third-grade class, "How many of you want to go to heaven?"

Everyone raised their hand except Billy. Sister said, "Billy, don't you want to go to heaven?"

Billy said, "No, Sister, not if all of them are going!"

We Had No Choice, We Had to Steal the Wine

When I was fifteen I went away to the seminary in upstate New York. It was an eye-opening experience. The fathers who ran the school had a mansion on Lake Shore Drive. They would recruit kids from Chicago and send them to New York. They must be the only missionaries in the Catholic Church who did not take the vow of poverty. They had fishing boats and Cadillacs and at least twice a month beer trucks would come up and unload. Of course, we never got the beer. We had to steal the sacramental wine.

—*Jay Constable, St. Gertrude's parish, Chicago, Illinois*

The Beer Bottle Toss

I went to the University of Notre Dame from 1959 to 1963. It would be comparable to West Point or Annapolis in terms of how strict things were. It was lights out at ten o'clock; they pulled the circuit breaker in the basement and they had bed check. The only lights left on were in the bathrooms. I remember seeing guys with their heads in the urinals studying. They allowed you one midnight a week to stay out. As a freshman you couldn't get caught drinking—you would be thrown flat out of school.

The first time I had any beer was maybe in November of my freshman year. We joined the Knights of Columbus because they had a bar; that was the only reason we joined. I was coming back to Farley Hall with a friend. The priests would always be there just watching to see if anyone had been drinking. We were stumbling drunk making our way to the dorm. We could see the priests hovering around like vultures. My friend threw a beer bottle through a stained-glass window in the chapel. It caused incredible havoc. All the priests ran into the chapel and we ducked into the dorm. I don't think I've ever been more frightened in my life. If we had been caught we would have been shot or dismembered, and gone straight to hell.

—*Dave Roberts, St. Joseph's parish, Wilmette, Illinois*

Punishment Brings Friends Together

We had serious uniform checks: length of the skirt, the blouse had to be white, it had to be pressed, and it had to have a collar. Gauze and Indian shirts were really popular and we were always trying to get away with wearing them. If you got caught the punishment was to be taken out of your classes and sent to the library to copy from the encyclopedias all day long. I'd call my girlfriend and say, "Let's wear our Indian shirts tomorrow, Suzanne." We would get to be together in the "encyclopedia room" all day.

—*C. Kimberly Regan, Holy Spirit parish, Stamford, Connecticut*

Bad Case of Hay Fever Gets Student Suspended

Tommy Barrios had the loudest sneeze in the world. The plan was, we would all put our books on the upper right-hand corner of our desks and when Tommy Barrios sneezed (because the whole school could hear it) we would all push our books off the desk. Tommy sneezed, we all shoved our books on the floor, and the nuns thought there was an earthquake. All the nuns ran into the hallways and Sister Joan of Arc fell apart. Tommy Barrios was suspended. He said, "Sister, all I did was sneeze!"

—*Rosemary D. Wesela, Saints Peter and Paul parish, Milwaukee, Wisconsin*

The priest opened the confessional and bumped into Johnny with his ear pressed up against the door.

"Johnny," said the priest, "were you eavesdropping again?"

"No, Father," said Johnny, "I didn't hear anything about that girl screwing the janitor."

Red Pencil Revenge

In my sophomore year in high school, the nun who taught English insisted that we had to have red pencils to correct each other's papers. Not just any red pencils but special red pencils that she would sell to us to for a quarter. We all paid our quarter to "purchase" the pencils. It was more like a rental fee; we didn't really own them. Every time we corrected each other's paper's the nun would pass out the red pencils and then collect them back. She kept them in a little box in her desk. We were not allowed to take the pencils home with us. At the end of the year Mary Lou Donohue asked the nun, "Sister, what about those pencils? I want mine. I paid for it." The nun said, "Oh no, I have to keep them here." Mary Lou said, "What about the money?" Sister said, "It went to a good cause. I gave the money to the missions." The next day Mary Lou came into the classroom before Sister arrived. She took the box of "rented" red pencils and threw them out the window, to the cheers of the class.

—*Patricia Kowal West, St. Leo's parish, Chicago, Illinois*

6

CATHOLIC HIGH SCHOOL CLASSICS

It could be an anecdote about the time someone put a whoopie cushion on Sister Mary Crucifix's chair or when Brother Ignatius O'Reilly threw the algebra book at the pigeons on the windowsill. We love to tell and retell the stories of our high school exploits. Some of these tales have reached the status of legendary classics.

The Miraculous Sparkler Plant

This really old nun taught Spanish class. Out of boredom, Gail Moran asked the nun why she kept a dead plant on the windowsill. The nun said, "One day, my child, God will perform a miracle and the plant will come back to life." A few days later Gail saw someone with a sparkler. A lightbulb went on in her head. She went to the nursery and bought a healthy green plant. While the nun was writing on the blackboard,

Gail put a sparkler in the verdant green plant and switched it with the one that was old and dried up. Gail yelled, "Hermana, hermana, the miracle has happened!" The nun turned around and saw the pyrotechnics of the miraculous houseplant and threw herself prostrate on the floor. Gail removed the sparkler and kept a low profile for about a week.

—*Jill Kowal Stanley, St. Leo's parish, Chicago, Illinois*

Another Catholic Rite of Passage

Bishop Egan was the first Catholic high school in Bucks County. The teachers were priests, TORs—Franciscan Third-Order Regulars (I'm not sure if they had irregulars). The TORs wore those long robes with cords at the waist. These cords could be used as a very effective weapon. Our school was coinstitutional (coed but the boys and girls went to separate classes). The school was just outside Philadelphia. There were gangs and lots of crime in the city high schools but our suburban school was pretty tame. But the Franciscans wanted to keep a lid on any potential violence. They were very big on avoiding chair throwing in the cafeteria. Our school cafeteria had these weird tables. They were bolted to the ground and the attached seats swung out from underneath the table. I saw a similar table once in a prison movie. Besides preventing unwanted violence they were also very big on preventing unwanted pregnancies. The school kept the sexes apart at all times; we didn't even eat lunch together. Actually everyone was kept apart. The priests had their own dining room so they could gossip about the students and smoke Camel cigarettes in peace. They left us alone during lunch. This was probably a big mistake.

When things got boring, the seniors would start pounding on the lunch tables: tap, tap, tap-tap-tap, tap-tap-tap-tap, TAP-TAP. This was the rhythm beat of a popular rock song called "Let's Go!" by the Routers. Then, the juniors, wanting to be cool, would chime in: tap, tap, tap-tap-tap, tap-tap-tap-tap,

TAP-TAP. The sophomores and freshmen wanted to imitate the upperclassmen so they would also start pounding. Hundreds of teens in unison: tap, tap, tap-tap-tap, tap-tap-tap-tap, TAP-TAP. The sound was thunderous; you could hear it up on the third floor. The priests would come running into the lunchroom with cigarettes dangling from their mouths. They didn't know what was going on but they were convinced it was something illegal. The seniors who started this madness were always the first to spot the priests. The crafty seniors would throw up their hands over their heads to show the priests they were just innocent bystanders. And the juniors would use the same ploy. Like crazed Cossacks the priests would run past the seniors and juniors sitting at their prison tables. Then the priests would start swinging. They would hit row after row of the underclassmen with their lethally knotted waist cords.

—Bill Dolon, *Our Lady of Grace parish, Penndel, Pennsylvania*

Buttons for the Missions

Sister Josaphat had a wart on the end of her tongue. She'd flick her tongue when she talked. "Girls (flick, flick), today we are collecting for the missions (flick, flick)." She passed the box around and everyone put in a penny except my best friend Terri Walowski. Terri twisted a button off her sweater and put it in the missions box." Sister Josaphat opened the box and said, "All right (flick, flick), who put the button in the mission box?" No one owned up. The next day Sister said, "Come on, girls, take that dime you are saving for a candy bar (flick, flick) and put it in the missions box." She found another button in the missions box. Still no one would tell who put the button in the box. All week, Sister Josaphat found a single button in with the change money. Finally, she figured out that it must be the girl who only had one button left on her five-button sweater: Terri Walowski. On the fifth day she said, "Miss Walowski (flick, flick), I believe you owe the missions a dollar." Terri stood up and said, "I don't think so, Sister." Sister Josaphat said, "How many buttons (flick, flick) do you have on your sweater?" Terri said, "I only have one, Sister." Sister Josaphat looked at her and said, "That's because (flick, flick) I haven't passed the missions box yet today."

—*Joann Boyle, St. Walter's parish, Chicago, Illinois*

Lettering in Fundraising

Every year the brothers who ran my high school had a fundraising drive to collect money to run their seminary so they could make more brothers. All the students were required to go out and collect money. They called it the LaSalle Club. I don't know why—maybe it was named for some Bishop LaSalle. The fundraiser had a quota. You were expected to collect at least fifteen dollars—that was the minimum. If you reached certain levels you received different kinds of recognition. The ultimate was a hundred dollars. If you managed to collect a hundred dollars they gave you a varsity letter to wear on your school sweater. This was one of the few schools where you could actually letter in fundraising. Totally nerdy guys got the exact same letter as the members of the basketball team. You couldn't tell the difference by just looking at their sweaters. Nerds were walking around school with a varsity letter because they had collected a hundred dollars for the seminary. Even cool guys would wear the fundraising letter. Imagine the guys who were on the basketball team and got a letter in fundraising too. They probably grew up to be very tall financial planners.

—*Michael Iapoce, St. Mary's parish, Long Island City, Queens, New York*

Mr. Rat Piss

I went to a Jesuit high school, Loyola Academy. We had a lay teacher who was brutal. Our first teacher lasted about six weeks and then he was drafted. He was nice and easy. We would pass our papers across the aisle and correct each other's work; of course we all got 100s. Then Mr. Nice-guy left. His replacement looked mean. His first day on the job, he was standing with his back to the class and writing very, very slowly on the blackboard, M-r. R-A-T-H-M-I-S. Immediately everybody thought to themselves "Mr. Rat Piss." He turned around and introduced himself: "I am Mr. Rathmis." He was very deliberate and slow. Some guy from the back of the class said, "Rat Piss." Mr. Rathmis just kept talking and slowly walked down the aisle—didn't give any hint of what was coming. Well, he just creamed this guy. He really decked him. Mr. Rathmis picked the right guy, the absolute troublemaker. Everyone just went "Ahhhh." There was a hush over the class. There wasn't a peep the rest of the semester.

—*Dave Roberts, St. Joseph's parish, Wilmette, Illinois*

Saint Dubrit

In high school there was a group of us at a party drinking the soft drink Sprite. We were acting silly and rearranged the letters from the word *Sprite* and came up with the word *Dubrit*. The *du* was French for "from the"; the *brit* was the "p" turned upside-down to make a "b" and the "s" and "e" dropped off.

At the time, we were taking a class in church history and thought the word *Dubrit* sounded like a saint's name. We made him the patron saint of the etymology of the discourse of teenagers; in other words, the patron saint of slang. He was from Avila overlooking the home where Saint Theresa was born (the party happened to be at a home in Saint Theresa's parish). As the party went on we made up a whole history about this imaginary Saint Dubrit.

We asked our religion teacher, Sister Mary Edward, if we could do a panel discussion on Saint Dubrit for our church history class. Sister didn't recognize St. Dubrit's name, but she was cool and said okay. Four of us did a forty-five-minute panel on the life and times of Saint Dubrit. Sister Mary

Edward never said a word. That was our punishment—she never let on that she knew that Saint Dubrit was a total sham. We were anticipating being expelled for our terrible crime. The next year we celebrated Saint Dubrit's feast day. I can't remember the date but I know it wasn't April 1.

  —*Rory (Rosemary) Keller, St. William's parish, Cincinnati, Ohio*

7

SERVING AT THE ALTAR

"God bless you lad, forever. And keep you in His care, and guard that you may never belie the robes you wear." Wise counsel from Saint John Berchman, the patron of altar boys. But let's face it—in today's church, altar "boys" are often girls. Things have changed since Saint John Berchman's time and so we offer a contemporary view of the altar service business.

The priest is about to baptize the baby. He asks the godmother, "What's the child's name?"

"Steven John Patrick Kevin William Andrew Carl Winston III."

The priest says to the altar boy, "More water, please."

Father Fitz vs. the Pigeons

Father James Fitzpatrick, to any kid under the age of twelve, was the very paragon of terror; he was the kind of adult who seemed dour, overly religious, and more liable to swat you than speak to you. He was bald, big, bespectacled, and when he smiled, it seemed an austere sort of grin. But once you turned thirteen, you realized that none of these things were true. In fact, despite my disinterest in being a man of the cloth, I find I'm becoming more and more like Father Fitz—I'm not much interested in children under the age of twelve.

If you were over thirteen, though, Father Fitz was a blast. I remember at a church youth dance, where he was one of the chaperones, I saw him confiscate a flask of something from a high school boy, take a sip from it, look refreshed, and hand it back to the boy saying, "Don't let me see this again for the rest of the night." The guy must have died of fright during the sampling of his wares.

The fondest memory I have of Father Fitzpatrick, though, is his preparation for mass while we altar boys got into our holier-than-we-were cassocks. There was a narrow green between the sacristy, where the priest vested himself, and the rectory, the priest's house, and in that space was a statue of the Virgin Mary, fairly large and usually adorned with a couple of laurel wreaths.

The problem was that the Virgin Mary's laurels were perfect places for pigeons to nest, and she was constantly bespattered with guano and molted feathers. Father Fitz would curse the birds, despite Saint Francis, in the most religious of words.

Words were not enough. So one day, as we prepared for noon mass, and I was polishing the patens and the two other altar boys were slipping on their robes, Father Fitzpatrick pulled from among his vestments a Smith and Wesson double-barreled shotgun, opened the window onto the green, aimed at the head of the Virgin Mary, and fired shots that could be heard in the soundproof confessional booths on the other side of the church.

What I remember most was the dead pigeon, at the foot of the Blessed Virgin, one foot up and three toes splayed in a perfect image of the crucifix. Father Fitz said a small prayer. A very small one. And then he led us through the back of the church so that we could lead the processional to mass.

—*Brian Bouldrey, author of* The Genius of Desire *and former altar boy, St. Mary's Star of the Sea parish, Jackson, Michigan*

Altar boys Mike and Bill were serving mass one Sunday. Mike whispered to Bill during the sermon, "Looks like we got a lot of golfers in here this morning." Bill whispered back, "Really, how can you tell?" "It's easy," said Mike, "when they put their hands together to pray they use an interlocking grip."

The Altar Boy Play-Offs

There was a certain undercurrent of competition that was part of the religious community. For example, it was a big deal to be selected to be an altar server at confirmation because the bishop would preside over the ceremony. I knew my Latin and was well behaved so Father Stevens chose me. At confirmation there were always priests from neighboring parishes in attendance. Naturally, there was a lot of pressure to do everything perfectly. You didn't want to embarrass your parish priests. It was a big deal to see who had the best altar boys. In the sacristy the other priests would say things like, "So, what are you teaching these boys? They didn't look so good out there." If you couldn't perform on the altar it was like losing a high school basketball game. You were letting the team down.

When I was in eighth grade, I was about 5 feet 8 inches and weighted about 11 pounds—very skinny. My job at the confirmation ceremony was to wash the bishop's hands. Normally at mass they had those tiny cruets but for confirmation they had a huge pitcher. The bishop had to wash off the oily chiasm. There I was this scrawny guy kneeling down and holding an enormous pitcher and my hand started to shake. It was just too heavy. The bishop came over and I poured the water but I couldn't control it. The water went all over the

bishop's sleeves and on the floor. Father Stevens was mortified. And the other priests were thinking, "We won, we won!"
—*Richard Kelleher, former altar boy, Sacred Heart parish,*
East Grand Forks, Minnesota

Billy the rookie altar boy is serving his first wedding. The priest pronounces the couple man and wife. He says, "You may kiss the bride." The groom lifts the bride's veil and kisses his new wife.

Billy says to the other altar boy, "Is this where he sprinkles pollen on her?"

That's a Gyp

My son Christopher was an altar boy. He loved working funerals because he could make some money. After a requiem mass, the funeral director handed the priest an envelope with the tips for the altar boys. The boys all knew how much money each of the different funeral directors doled out. Black and Lum's always gave a ten-dollar tip for each of the altar boys. After a Black and Lum's funeral, the pastor of the church called the boys into the sacristy and handed them each a single dollar for serving the mass. Christopher came home and said, "That's it, he took our money. No more altar boy for me."
—*Joann Boyle, St. Walter's parish, Chicago, Illinois*

Father Kelly is hearing confessions during Easter week and the church is jammed. One of the altar boys, Billy, kneels in the confessional and the priest says, "Look, Billy, it's so busy. I'm just going to give you absolution without hearing your sins; that is, unless you've committed murder in the past week."

As Billy is leaving the confessional he runs into his buddy Jack. "Don't bother going in. He's only hearing murder cases."

Unorthodox Advice from Former Altar Boys and Girls

MAKING A CLEAN BREAST OF IT

I was serving a wedding. It was my job to fill that holy water sprinkler thing—I've forgotten the name of it. I was in a hurry and I got it on crooked. When it came time for the priest to bless the bride the top flew off and hit her right in the chest. The front of her gown was soaked.

Always screw the top on tightly.

—*Joe Weatherby, former altar boy, Our Lady of Mercy parish,*
Sarnia, Ontario, Canada

NOT EXACTLY MUSIC TO MY EARS

I hated serving mass during Lent because the rule was you had to fast before communion. Early mass with the nuns was the worst! They must have fasted for days. I could hear their stomachs growling and gurgling all the way up on the altar.

If you have to serve mass with fasting nuns, wear earplugs.

—*Dan Shaughnessy, former altar boy, Sacred Heart parish,*
Groton, Massachusetts

AND IT WORKS IF YOU'RE A POLITICIAN TOO

They were still saying the mass in Latin just before I became an altar boy. I asked my older brother, "How do you learn the Latin?" He said, "No problem, kid. When you get up to the altar you just mumble."

—*Tom Kole, St. Leo's parish, Chicago, Illinois*

STRANGERS ONLY

I served the mass for the First Holy Communion class. My sister Jill was making her communion that day. I got nervous when I saw her kneeling at the altar ready to receive the host. I accidentally hit her in the throat with the palette. The priest gave me a quick little whack for hitting her.

Never serve mass when you know your relatives will be there.

—*Peter Kowal, former altar boy, St. Leo's parish, Chicago, Illinois*

WANDERING AROUND IN THE DARK

When I had to light the candles before a big mass, I refused to wear my glasses in front of people. I couldn't see. I'd be out there for ten or fifteen minutes trying to light the candles with that long stick. Finally, someone would come out and rescue me.

If you wear glasses, put your glasses on for candle-lighting purposes.

—*Dave Roberts, former altar boy, St. Joseph's parish, Wilmette, Illinois*

ALTAR-GATOR TEARS

Whenever I was serving at a funeral, I would always swing the censer so the incense would get into my eyes and make me cry. The big tears running down my checks would guarantee an extra big tip from the bereaved family.

—*Tom Watkins, former altar boy, Holy Angels parish, Arcadia, California*

I JUST DO IT FOR THE MONEY

My buddy Michael Webber and I were side-servers at a high requiem mass. During the consecration he stuck me in the leg with a pin. Naturally, I yelled out. The nun in charge of the altar boys, Sister Cosmas, found out and booted both of us out of the altar boy corps. At first I was totally humiliated. Then it dawned on me that I wouldn't have to get up at 6 A.M. to serve mass during summer vacation. Getting kicked out was the best thing that could have happened to me! As luck would have it, Mrs. Webber pleaded my case to Sister Cosmas and I was reinstated. Like most nuns, Sister Cosmas knew how to hold a grudge. After that incident she never assigned me to serve at a wedding. Wedding services were very coveted among altar boys because you always got a tip.

Be sure to serve as many weddings as you can. That's where the money is!

—*Jack Kowal, former altar boy, St. Leo's parish, Chicago, Illinois*

GOD SEES YOU NO MATTER WHERE YOU THROW UP

I was never what you would call a model altar boy. One morning I got up early to serve 7 A.M. mass and I wasn't feeling very good. I was kneeling on the altar when a wave of nausea hit me. I made a run for the bathroom but didn't quite make it. I threw up in front of the priest, God, and the four little old ladies who were at mass that morning.

If you are feeling sick, stay home!

—*Peter Butler, former altar boy, Immaculate Conception parish,*
Elmhurst, Illinois

THEY'RE JUST SO MELLOW

I always wanted to serve mass with the priests who drank a lot of wine during mass. They were the easiest to work with.

—*Daniel Hernandez, former altar boy, Holy Family parish,*
San Antonio, Texas

LOVE THOSE LEFTOVERS

My favorite extracurricular activity as an altar boy was to drink the leftover wine in the priest's chalice after mass. It was a mystery to us where they kept the wine supply. When we were setting up before mass the cruets were always full. It would arouse suspicion to ask about the wine. I'd love to know what kind of wine they used.

Always check the chalice for any leftovers.

—*Craig Bashel, former altar boy, American Martyrs parish,*
Manhattan Beach, California

The Last Word

Mission District teenager Gabrielle Muzac, an altar girl at Saint Anthony of Padua Church, has some advice for Pope John Paul II.

"My dad showed me an article that said the pope doesn't believe women should serve at the altar. I couldn't believe it," said Gabrielle, age fifteen. "We've been doing it here for so long. Are they just finding out now? You don't have to be a man to serve God."

—San Francisco Chronicle

8

UNHOLY BODILY FUNCTIONS

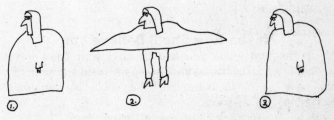

THE FLATULENT NUN

Callahan

The sisters impressed on us that our bodies are "temples of the Holy Ghost." They failed to mention, however, that our bodies are occasionally subject to some rather unholy malfunctions.

What Kind of Response Is That?

My brother was an altar boy at St. Mary's Cathedral in the seventies. One of the other altar boys was particularly flatulent. They were both kneeling on the altar and he let out a rip-roaring fart, at least thirty seconds long. We were all thankful for the incense that morning.

—*Agnes Consolacion, St. Mary's Cathedral, San Francisco, California*

What Was Your Confirmation Name . . . Queezie?

The morning of my confirmation I was nervous and didn't want to eat. During the service it was very hot in the church. The ceremony seemed to take forever; the bishop talked for hours. Finally, it was my turn to go up and be confirmed. The bishop, assisted by the parish priest, confirmed me with the holy chrism. As he was confirming the next boy in line, I threw up all over the bishop. The boy started crying. I said, "Why are you crying? I'm the one that's sick."

—*Richard Boyle, St. Adrian's parish, Chicago, Illinois*

What do they call bathrooms in Rome?
Vati-Cans.

Maybe Now She'll Believe You

In the first grade you had to raise your hand if you wanted to go to the bathroom. I raised my hand and said, "Sister, I have to go to the bathroom." She yelled, "No you don't!" So I crapped in my pants.

—*Tom Kole, St. Leo's parish, Chicago, Illinois*

Not Unless You Aimed at Mother Superior

Every Friday afternoon the nuns would line us up and march us into church for confession. I had the awful liability of being a perfect child so I never had any good sins. There was a group of us who would maneuver our way to the end of the line so we could discuss which sins we should confess. "Is spitting a sin?" "I don't know. Say it anyway."

—*Marie Aranas, Sacred Heart parish, San Francisco, California*

The Well-Dressed Fainter

My First Holy Communion I was very excited and very nervous. You couldn't eat anything the night before or that morning. There I was all dressed up in my white dress, the veil, the little white ruffled socks, the white shoes, the missile and rosary beads. I was just getting into the pew and my knees buckled and I went down, passed out.

—*Susan Santos, St. Genevieve's parish, Van Nuys, California*

Picky, Picky, Picky

We knew how to drive this one old nun crazy. We'd all put our fingers in our noses. She'd pound the desk and in a sing-song voice say, "Children, please don't pick your nose. It makes me sick."

—*Betty Czekala, Little Flower parish, Chicago, Illinois*

A little old lady wanders into the dark confessional. She is looking around in a state of utter confusion when the priest slides back the screen.

"Excuse me," says the old lady "you have lovely accommodations but before I use them do you have any toilet paper in your stall?"

The Day Sally Going Went

My third-grade nun Sister Rose used to go off on these tangents and talk and talk and talk. She'd tell us about the bombings in World War II or go on and on about the possibility of being taken over by the communists. When she'd get on a roll she didn't like to be interrupted.

Sally Going sat at the desk in front of me. One morning Sister Rose was telling us in great detail how to protect ourselves if Russia dropped the atomic bomb. Sally very meekly raised her hand. Sister said, "Please put your hand down." Sister was just getting to the part about how to crouch under our desks and cover our heads when Sally's hand went up again. "Sally," said Sister Rose, "I asked you not to interrupt." Sister started up again and reminded us not to look at the mushroom cloud when Sally's hand shot up in a very insistent manner. "Now you are being rude," said Sister Rose and continued on with her end-of-the-world drill and then Sally Going ... went! It was like a floodgate opened. I can still remember the sound like a great explosion of water. Dead silence in the room and then you could hear the drip, drip, drip. To her credit Sister Rose apologized to Sally.

—*Michele Canning, St. Etheldreda's parish, Chicago, Illinois*

9

THOU SHALT NOT . . .

Missing mass on Sunday? Wearing civilian clothes to parochial school? Eating meat on Good Friday? Dating that nice Jewish boy down the street? In addition to the Ten Commandments there were tons of things Catholics were not allowed to do.

Sandwich Inspection

We had spot "lunchbox checks" on Fridays, just to make sure your mother didn't accidentally make you a roast beef sandwich. If the nuns found any meat they turned over the sandwich to the convent and the housekeeper would make a replacement tuna sandwich.

—*Kathy McGilvery, St. Brendan's parish, San Francisco, California*

Whatever Happened to Ecumenicalism?

On Friday afternoons at the local park gym they had dances for the eighth-grade students. All the Our Lady of Mercy kids would be on one side of the gym and all the Bateman Public School kids on the other. We never, never cross-danced.

—*Cheryl K. Hylton, Unitarian, Chicago, Illinois*

But Sister, He's the King!

When we collected five dollars for the missions our class would choose a name for the pagan baby we had "purchased." I always wanted to name the pagan baby Elvis but the nun wouldn't let me.

—*Rick Kelleher, Sacred Heart parish, East Grand Forks, Minnesota*

Just a Reminder

When I made my First Holy Communion we were not allowed to drink water from midnight on. The morning of my First Communion my mother had a towel draped across the sink so I wouldn't forget.

—*Patricia Kowal West, St. Leo's parish, Chicago, Illinois*

Unsanctioned Playmates

Growing up I was not allowed to play with Protestants. In my Catholic family it was believed the only true religions were Catholic and Jewish. No other religion was true. My family believed that those people just made up those other religions for their own convenience.

—*Margaret Komet Hensley, Saints Simon and Jude parish,*
Brooklyn, New York

10

FURTHER PROOF THAT GOD IS A CATHOLIC

These reports from sources around the country serve as yet more evidence to prove what every Catholic knows to be true.

Free Auto Insurance from Bronx Grotto

A shrine dedicated to Our Lady at Saint Lucy's in the Bronx is a replica of the French grotto where the Virgin Mary appeared to Bernadette Soubirous in 1858. As reported by the *New York Times*, many claim to have been cured by the New York City waters that have been blessed by St. Lucy's parish priest. In addition to the curative powers of the holy waters, many of the believers use the water to bless their Chevys and BMWs. Owners park their new autos outside the Bronx grotto and haul buckets of water curbside. The faithful wash their cars in the blessed waters to protect them from harm.

God rewards his faithful with perks such as no-cost auto insurance.

Don't Mess with John Paul II

Never underestimate the power of the pontiff: Monday night, a scene for *Significant Other*, starring Andy Garcia and Meg Ryan, was about to be shot on the third floor of Saints Peter and Paul in North Beach. There were thirty-three actors there for an Alcoholics Anonymous meeting (Meg plays an alky), and the cameraman kept getting a glare from the photo of Pope John Paul II. The director put it out in the hall and shooting resumed? No, it did not. All three cameras went dead. The photo was put back on the wall but they still wouldn't work, so the shooting was called off.

From Herb Caen's column in the San Francisco Chronicle

Virgin Mary Scoops CNN
FATIMA FEVER: DID MARY PROPHESY SOVIET GOINGS-ON?
Believers Say Blessed Virgin Beat CNN to the News by More Than 74 Years

—Headline in the Wall Street Journal

The article in the *Wall Street Journal* recounts the events of Our Lady's appearance at Fatima to three Portuguese shepherd children in May 1917. The Blessed Mother revealed to the children that the Soviet Union would cause great turmoil but would one day be converted to Catholicism through the prayer of believers.

History speaks for itself. As any parochial school child can tell you, the USSR created its fair share of havoc and the evil empire has fallen. Not only did the Blessed Virgin scoop CNN, but these events were prophesied twenty-one years before the news network's owner Ted Turner, a non-Catholic, was born.

Jesus Is a Notre Dame Fan

As any died-in-the-Irish-wool Notre Dame fan can tell you, "Touchdown Jesus" is the image of Christ on the mural in the University's Memorial Library. The actual title of the mural is "The Word of Life." Jesus, surrounded by apostles, saints, and scholars, is represented in the work as "Christ the Teacher." The 132-foot-tall granite mural—which can been seen from the Notre Dame football stadium—depicts Our Savior with his arms uplifted. Not long after the library was dedicated in 1964, the granite mosaic of Our Lord was given the nickname

"Touchdown Jesus." Although He's not dressed in black and white stripes, it would appear that the mosaic Jesus is signaling for a touchdown. The looming presence of Touchdown Jesus has put the "Fear of God" into more than one opponent of the Fighting Irish.

ND fans have speculated that Touchdown Jesus's winning influence has been translated into cold cash for their football team. A *Business Week* article stated that the Fighting Irish signed an unprecedented $38-million-plus five-year television broadcast contract with NBC in 1990. Notre Dame is the only major university to have its own network-TV contract.

The Score: Bishop Fulton J. Sheen I, Joseph Stalin 0

In the 1950s Bishop Fulton J. Sheen, a staunch anticommunist, was seen coast-to-coast on his popular weekly television show, "Life Is Worth Living." In 1953 the charismatic bishop delivered a dramatic reading of the burial scene from Shakespeare's Julius Caesar. As reported in *The Complete Directory to Prime Time Network TV Shows 1946–Present* by Tim Brooks and Earle Marsh, Bishop Sheen substituted the names of Caesar, Cassius, Marc Anthony, and Brutus with Stalin, Beria, Malenkov, and Vishinsky. The Catholic bishop looked into the camera and said, "Stalin must one day meet his judgment."

A few days later Joseph Stalin suffered a sudden stroke and died the following week. While this remarkable "coincidence" was widely reported in the press, there was never any comment from the modest Bishop Sheen.

They Play Bingo in Heaven

A Chicago secretary, Anna Danell, suffered a massive heart attack while she and her seven-year-old son were visiting Spain. As reported in an article in the *Weekly World News*, Anna was pronounced dead by Dr. Manuel Dominguez. Her body was about to be taken to the morgue when she woke up and a Bingo card mysteriously appeared in her hand.

Danell, an avid Bingo player, was said to have played Bingo twice a week for the past twenty years. Reportedly, Danell floated toward a bright light and found herself playing Bingo with her dead mother in a "special place." Anna won the Bingo game and the Bingo angels were about to give her the fifty-dollar prize money when she said, "You keep the fifty bucks, but let me take my card home as a souvenir." Then she woke up in the hospital with the winning Bingo card in her hand.

Holy Family Spared in the Great Chicago Fire

The Great Chicago Fire destroyed a significant portion of the Windy City but Holy Family Catholic Church at Roosevelt Road and May Street was spared by the terrible blaze. Today at the church seven candles are constantly lit in front of the statue of the Virgin Mary as a reminder of this historic and miraculous event. According to the book *Holy Family Parish Chicago: Priests and People* by Brother Thomas J. Mulkerins, S. J., the fire started on October 8, 1871, within blocks of Holy Family. A gusty wind blowing in the direction of the church almost ensured its total destruction. The pastor, Father Arnold Damen, was holding a mission in Brooklyn when the fire broke out. His quick-thinking assistant telegraphed the priest to inform him of the grave danger his beloved church faced. Father Damen was hearing confessions at Saint Patrick's. When the note was handed to him, he immediately went to the altar and prayed all night that his church would be saved. Father Damen vowed to the Blessed Mother that if Holy Family was spared, forever more seven lights would burn in front of the statue of the *Lady of Perpetual Help*. The wind shifted and drove the fire away from Holy Family and went on to destroy the entire downtown Chicago.

Nun Wins Popularity Contest

God works in mysterious ways. Surely it was a sign from above that topping the list of *Good Housekeeping*'s Twentieth Annual Most Admired Women Poll was Mother Teresa of Calcutta.

11

S — X: THE FORBIDDEN TOPIC

There are two types of sex: non-Catholic sex and Catholic sex. Non-Catholic sex is the physical union of two sweaty bodies. Catholic sex, as we learned in parochial school, is thinking about it, talking about it, postponing it, agonizing about it, feeling guilty about it, and confessing it. But never, never actually doing it.

Catholic Girls Are Hussies

My girlfriend went to Catholic school. It wasn't until I was an adult that I realized it was the Catholic school girls who were the first to smoke and the first to drink. And they were much more boy crazy than the girls from public schools.

Now, when I'm waiting at the bus stop in the morning with the schoolchildren, I see this young girl who wears a Catholic school uniform. Every morning her father drops her off. The minute her father pulls away she rolls up her skirt and gets out her cigarettes. She just stands there puffing away. You just know that when she gets a block from her school, she'll roll her skirt back down and hide her cigarettes.

—*Mary Regan, no religious affiliation, Livermore, California*

Two Catholics, Mike and Pat, are drinking in a bar across the street from a house of prostitution. They are watching the constant stream of customers go into the house. First they see the minister from the Methodist Church ring the doorbell.

"Wouldn't you know it," says Pat, "those Methodists are all alike."

Then Mike spots the pastor of the Lutheran Church sneaking into the bordello.

"Can you believe those Lutherans? They're all sex maniacs!" Mike says.

Next the rabbi from the local synagogue knocks on the door.

"Even the Jews are tempted by the flesh," says Pat.

Finally Father Riley from Most Holy Redeemer rings the doorbell.

They watch in amazed silence; then Mike turns to Pat and says, "How sad, one of the girls must be sick."

The Sex Diet

I think of prudence as a form of dieting. If I want to be thin, I avoid sweets. If I want to be holy, I avoid sex. To reduce the temptation to snack, I don't buy cookies and ice cream. Similarly, I avoid sexually explicit movies and novels to reduce the temptation to commit sexual sin. I decline the sexual advances of a date because it is too hard to eat just one potato chip and stop.

—Sex, Intimacy, and the Single Christian *by Martha M. Niemann,*
Liguori Publications

Too Many Kum-Ba-Ya's

We had a priest in our parish and a parishioner that ran off together and got married. He was the one who started the hootenanny masses. I guess there were too many Kum-Ba-Ya's going on.

—*Madelyn Johnson, Our Lady of the Ridge parish,*
Chicago Ridge, Illinois

First the Rosary, Then the Boys

I grew up across the street from Vickie DeAngelo. I was in the second grade and she was in the first grade. Vickie was Catholic and she told me all about being a Catholic. She gave me her rosary beads and taught me all the prayers. When Vickie stayed overnight, we would get down on our knees and say all the Hail Mary's, the Our Father's, the Glory Be's . . . and we'd see who could get say the rosary the fastest. If you finished first you'd say, "I won!" Then we would talk about boys.

—*Patricia Duff, Protestant, Denver, Colorado*

A newlywed went to confession and said to the priest, "Father, is it all right if my husband and I have intercourse before we receive communion?"

"Certainly, my child," said the priest, "just as long as you don't make too much noise."

Or, At Least Engaged

One of the little boys asked our catechism teacher, Father Dwyer, if a girl could get pregnant if she was only twelve.

Father was hemming and hawing because the nun was standing there. One of the other kids saved the day. He raised his hand and said, "It's not possible because she isn't married."

—*Betty Czekala, Little Flower parish, Chicago, Illinois*

Contour Tablecloths?

Sister Virginia told us if we went out to dinner on a date to be sure and avoid restaurants that had white tablecloths. They reminded boys of bed sheets and gave them ideas.

—*Michele Canning, St. Etheldreda's parish, Chicago, Illinois*

A nun dies and goes to heaven. Saint Peter greets her at the Pearly Gates and tells her, "We weren't expecting you so early. You'll have to go back to earth for a couple of weeks."

The nun calls Saint Peter and says, "This is Sister Gertrude. I'm fine; I got an apartment in Manhattan. But, I have to confess, the other day I had a drink in a bar."

Peter says, "Don't worry about it. Call me in three weeks." The time passes and he gets another call. "Saint Peter, this is Sister Gertrude. Is it time yet? Oh, by the way, I went dancing with some new friends."

"We're not ready for you yet. Don't worry about the dancing. Call next week."

Tuesday arrives and there's a message on the answering machine. "Pete, this is Gertie. Let's just forget the whole thing."

You Can't Fool Me

One time I confessed a homosexual experience so I disguised my voice. I confessed the sin of "bad actions with another." The priest asked who I committed the sin with. I thought, "Slide the other screen, Father. He's over there." But the joke of it was, after disguising my voice, as I left the confessional the priest said, "Joe, how's your mother?"

—*Joe Weatherby, Our Lady of Mercy parish, Sarnia, Ontario, Canada*

Two nuns are sitting on an airplane bound for Rome. The man sitting in the aisle across from them orders martini after martini. Finally, he leans across the aisle and propositions one of the sisters. Clutching her prayer book she leans across the aisle and says, "I've got news for you. You're going straight to hell!"

The drunk jumps up and yells, "Good God, I'm on the wrong flight."

Where to See a Woman's Breasts

My first experience of seeing a woman's breasts happened at a Catholic camp for boys. At nine years old, I was shipped out for the summer to Catholic camp in Riverside, California. It was the best thing since peanut butter! We lived in a dorm, had bugle calls in the morning, and had to go to mass every day. There I was at Catholic camp being holy and learning how to shoot rifles and box. All the saintly pursuits.

In the evenings they would show cheesy grade B movies that were dubbed. Movies like *Zapata and His Gang Rides.* All the older boys (who knew what was coming) got the good seats in the front row. The movies would get to a certain point where the main character, a Mexican stud, would grab the woman. He'd open her blouse and there they would be, dangling for everyone to see, these giant breasts.

—*Jonathan Yorba, Saint Martha's parish, La Puente, California*

Sister Bridget was asking the students in her seventh-grade class what they wanted to be when they grew up. Billy said, "Sister, I want to be a policeman."

"You'll make a grand policeman, Billy," said Sister Bridget.

"Sister," said Jane, "I want to be a nurse."

"That's a noble profession," said Sister Bridget.

"I want to be a prostitute," said Alice.

"Saints save us!" shrieked Sister Bridget. "You'll burn forever in hell."

"Just because I want to be a prostitute?"

"Thank the Lord," said Sister Bridget. "I thought you said 'Protestant.'"

A Non-Catholic Does Lent

I was raised a Methodist but I've always been a Catholic wanna-be. I never converted to Catholicism but I "do" Lent. I like the whole concept of Jesus being out in the wilderness eating twigs and bugs. Each year I give something up. The first year it was alcohol and the next year I gave up sex. My live-in boyfriend freaked out. He said, "Do we get to talk about this? Is this up for discussion?" I said, "No, not really." We aren't together anymore.

—*Inez Templeton, Methodist, Rocky Mount, North Carolina*

Measuring Up

We were supposed to wear full cotton leggings so our legs didn't show. In the summer you could wear knee-highs. There was a designated number of inches on how much leg could show. The nuns would measure us.

—*Margaret Komet Hensley, Saints Simon and Jude parish, Brooklyn, New York*

Two nuns are bicycling down a country road in France. One nun turns to the other and says, "I haven't come this way in a long time."

"Well, Sister," says the other, "maybe it's the cobblestones."

Comingling in High School

Our high school was coinstitutional. The boys were taught by the Christian Brothers and the girls had the Sisters of Mercy (so named because they had none). The school was shaped like a horseshoe. In one wing were the boys, in the other were the girls, and in the middle you had the cafeteria and the library. Those were the two areas we shared in common. At lunch the boys sat on one side of the cafeteria and the girls on the other. Only seniors were allowed to mingle with the opposite sex in the cafeteria. My friend once crossed the invisible line and was talking to a girl. One of the nuns started harassing him. He just said, "Don't bother me, Sister. I'm a senior." The idea of comingling was to keep our hormones in check. The nuns always tried to discourage us; it galled them that we had this privilege. Sometimes we had clandestine meetings with the girls in the library after school. Of course we couldn't talk.

There was this place we would meet after school—it was a Greek luncheonette. What an oddity, a Greek luncheonette in New York. That's where we would really comingle. We'd smoke cigarettes, drink chocolate egg-creams, order french fries, and spoil our dinner with a hamburger. Of course there would be periodic raids by the nuns and brothers because you weren't allowed to smoke within a block of the school. Brothers would suddenly swoop in and grab people.

—*Michael Iapoce, St Mary's parish, Long Island City, Queens, New York*

Why is it so difficult for religious orders to recruit young women to enter the convent?

Because they've all figured out that "nun" means "none."

That Priest Is a Hunk

In school we had this priest named Father Robert Malloy (who was probably about twenty-eight). He would say mass on occasion at our all-girl high school. That was the only time we all wanted to go to church. All the girls would say, "Oh boy, Malloy is saying mass." We'd all be fighting for the first pew. All of us wanted to take communion because *he* would put the wafer in our mouth. He was so good-looking we all wondered why he was a priest. A hunk gone to waste! We had this pretty teacher, who later became a nun. We all thought that the two of them should get together.

We thought Father Malloy was really gorgeous but without any standard of comparison it's hard to say. There were no other men around so we were starved for someone to look at. We would check out the men who painted the school and the guys who picked up the garbage.

—*Marie Aranas, Sacred Heart parish, San Francisco, California*

A man in London is rowing down the Thames when his oar falls into the water. He is drifting down the river when he spots a rowboat coming his way. In the rowboat are a man and two nuns. As the boat gets closer the man in the drifting boat yells, "Sir, will you lend me one of your oars?"

The man screams back, "They're not oars! They're sisters!"

A priest and a rabbi are enjoying a friendly game of chess when the priest says, "Tell me, Rabbi, have you ever tasted ham?"

The rabbi blushes. "To tell you the truth, I have. I was in college eating a sandwich that I thought was corned beef and, wouldn't you know, it was ham. But now it's your turn, Father. Tell me, have you ever been with a woman?"

"I have to be honest. Before I entered the priesthood, I must admit I had a few dates with a woman."

The rabbi smiles and says, "It's better than ham, isn't it?"

Streetwalkers

My eighth-grade nun was Sister Margaret Mary. Laurie Alioto and I used to walk home with the boys after school. Sister Margaret Mary called Laurie and me "women of the street."

—*Marcella Friel, St. Coleman's parish, Ardmore, Pennsylvania*

Three strangers met at a summer golf resort and decided to play together.

One guy introduced himself: "My name is Paul John, but I'm not the pope."

The other guy said, "My name is Matthew Mark, but I'm not a saint."

The woman said, "My n-n-name is M-m-m-mary, but I'm not a v-v-v-v-v-very good golfer."

Breaking the Vow of Silence

When I was in my twenties my cousin fixed me up with a guy who worked as a doorman in a singles bar. He told me he had been a monk and had just left the monastery. Being new to civilian life, he didn't have much experience with women. I thought he was a really nice guy but things just didn't work out between us. He talked too much.

—*Sally Starr, St. Louis parish, Chicago, Illinois*

A Purity Checklist

- Did I do anything that was really impure?
- Was it alone or with others?
- Did I willingly keep impure thoughts in my mind?
- Did I sin by using impure words?
- Did I sin by looking at or reading anything impure?
- Did I sin by talking about or listening to anything impure?

—Going to Confession *by Rev. L. Lovasik, S.V.D.*

"The Straight Dope" on Vatican Porn

Is it true that the Vatican has the world's most extensive collection of erotica and pornography locked away where no one can appreciate it (nor) can see it?—M.B., Baltimore

I have not had a chance to personally check this out, M., but I have spoken to others who have tried. Years ago a couple of researchers from the Kinsey Institute in Bloomington, Indiana, made an attempt to inspect the Vatican's collections, but church officials refused to permit it. Subsequently, however, it was learned that the Vatican had arranged to have its holdings microfilmed during World War II, when it was feared Rome would be bombed. The film is now stored in St. Louis University in Missouri. The Kinsey folks looked through all the material and found a few mildly erotic art items, but virtually nothing since the Renaissance. From this they concluded that stories about the Vatican's 100,000 books of porn are naught but a myth.

Not everyone buys this, of course; the more conspiracy-minded among us argue that the Vatican wouldn't be dumb enough to microfilm the smut section. One of my correspondents claims the Vatican library has (or had, anyway) thousands of erotic volumes, most of them file copies of works that appeared on the Catholic Church's well-known *Index of Prohibited Books*. This fellow says he spent time in a World War II concentration camp with a Vatican librarian, who gave him a tour of the library in 1945. He says many of the books, "mainly the illustrated volumes," have since disappeared.

Well, maybe. Most researchers, however, doubt that the Vatican has or ever had much genuine smut on the shelves. Gershon Legman, a prominent student of erotica who helped compile a bibliography of porn for Alfred Kinsey, says the Vatican "has no really erotic books," although there are some fairly tame volumes from the classical era. For instance, a copy of Ovid's *The Art of Love* is filed with Latin poetry, and Aristophanes' *Lysistrata* is with Greek drama. The Vatican also has some erotic specimens among its art holdings, including, among other things, some drawings by Michelangelo featuring various phallic fantasies. In addition there is a famous collection of erotic frescoes designed by Raphael in 1516 and executed by his students in the bathroom of Cardinal Bibbiena. The frescoes, which are badly deteriorated today, consist of scenes involving Venus and Cupid, Cupid and Psyche, and Vulcan and Pallas, and one would be hard put to describe them as even mildly titillating.

This is not to say that hard-core porn is unknown to Rome. A student of Raphael's by the name of Guilio Romano produced some quite explicit erotic art, in particular a series of twenty drawings depicting some rambunctious couplings, which were turned over to an engraver and printed up in book form. Pope Clement VII was outraged and had the engraver heaved into prison, but copies of the book continued to circulate clandestinely in Europe for centuries. Whether the Vatican has a copy today, I dunno, but they ought to—most good university art collections do.

As for the *Index of Prohibited Books* (which, by the way, was discontinued in 1966), I've taken a look at it, and you could probably come up with a racier bunch of titles in your average Woolworth's. About 1,500 books and/or authors are listed; of the small percentage alleged to be "obscene" (obscenity was just one of twelve categories of forbidden works, the remainder having to do with heresies and the like), many were written by such famous authors as Honoré de Balzac, Alexandre Dumas (both father and son), Emile Zola, Anatole France, and Victor Hugo. None of the erotic "classics" (e.g., *Fanny Hill*, the works of de Sade) were listed, maybe because the Vatican figured they were of such limited circulation they weren't worth worrying about.

In short, I think the legendary Vatican pornography collection is a crock. Most of the stories you hear about it are undoubtedly part of the folklore that surrounds any large, old, secretive institution (the Masons are another case in point). However, there are some truly awesome smut depots out there, if you're into that kind of thing. The Municipal Museum of Naples, for instance, is said to have an amazing collection of erotic artifacts, most of them classical in origin—fornicating satyrs and so forth. The British Museum in London has a famous "Private Case" collection of erotica bequeathed to it by eccentric Victorians that at one time was said to number 20,000 volumes, although theft, vandalism, and other causes have reduced it to somewhere between 1,800 and 5,000 volumes, depending on who's counting. In Paris the Bibiotheque Nationale's famous L'Enger ("hell") collection contains 4,000–5,000 volumes. What may be the largest collection of all is held by the Kinsey Institute (formally known as the Kinsey Institute for Research in Sex, Gender, and Reproduction) on the campus of Indiana University at Bloomington. There are some 12,000 books, 50,000 photographs, 25,000 pieces of flat art, 3,700 films, and 1,300 art objects, such as figurines. The collection spans the ages, but much of it is of recent origin. The fact is that color photography, the high-speed offset press, and more recently, the videocassettes have resulted in a profusion of erotica that makes the porn collections in Europe seem positively quaint.

—*From* The Straight Dope *by Cecil Adams*

12

SISTERS, MOTHERS, FATHERS, AND BROTHERS

As the members of the clergy fulfill their lofty roles as our teachers, spiritual guides, and administers of the sacraments, sometimes it is easy for us to forget that the clergy too are only human.

The Real Flying Nun

Sister Maxine was a Benedictine who taught physics at Cathedral High in St. Cloud, Minnesota, during the 1940s. A licensed pilot, Sister Maxine answered the call from Uncle Sam during World War II and instituted a class in aeronautics at Cathedral High. The idea was to familiarize the students with the basics of aviation.

In an article in *Catholic Digest* it was reported that Sister Maxine was asked if she said a prayer before takeoff. The high-flying sister responded, "Can't say that I do.... You don't say a special prayer every time you get into an automobile, do you?"

It's a beautiful day at Wrigley Field and two nuns are sitting in the bleachers watching the Cubs. Sitting behind the nuns are a couple of fans drinking beer. One of the guys says to his pal, "I can't see a thing. These nuns' hats are blocking the whole field. Remind me to move to San Francisco where only ten percent of the people are Catholic."

His friend says, "Let's move to Kansas City where only five percent are Catholic."

One of the nuns turns around and says, "Why don't you both go to hell. You won't find any Catholics."

The Blessing of the Gun

I am a police officer in the city of Chicago. When the pope was on his tour of the United States, I was put on bodyguard detail for all the cardinals who were staying at the Hilton Hotel. I wore a business suit, looking real good, keeping my eyes open for trouble. My partner (who was dressed in his uniform) was talking to one of the cardinals in the lobby. My partner intimated to the cardinal that his uncle was in organized crime. He introduced me to the cardinal and asked His Eminence if he would bless my gun. I was in street clothes and the cardinal thought I was the guy in organized crime. Later that evening my partner told me the circumstances of the cardinal's blessing. We got into a big argument. I thought the blessing didn't count because it was under false pretenses; the cardinal thought I was the Mafioso. Years later I asked a priest and he said, "Yes, the blessing counts."

—*Richard Boyle, St. Adrian's parish, Chicago, Illinois*

A priest is playing golf with a wealthy parishioner at a very exclusive country club just outside of Boston. As they are about to tee up the man says, "You realize, Father, if Jesus lived in Boston he couldn't belong to this club. His father was a carpenter."

The priest said, "Yes, but he had good connections on his mother's side."

The Keys to the Kingdom?

Brothers and nuns always have millions of keys. I don't know why. What have they got to lock up?

—*Michael Iapoce, St. Mary's parish, Long Island City, Queens, New York*

A priest buys two parrots and teaches them to say the rosary. After months of training, the birds are able to say the Hail Mary's, Our Father's, and Glory Be's in perfect order. The priest is so proud of the parrots that he has two tiny rosary beads made for the birds.

The priest decides to train another parrot to pray and goes to the pet store and buys a female parrot. He brings the parrot home and puts her in the cage with the other two birds.

One parrot turns to the other and says, "Throw away your rosary beads. Our prayers have been answered."

Priests Cash in When Saint Rita Helps to Win the Lottery

In 1975 my husband bought a fifty-cent ticket for the Illinois State Lottery. The numbers on his lottery ticket were pulled so he was one of those selected to play the horse race game. He went to work the next morning and gave me the ticket to go down and see if I could win. I got dressed that morning and wore a sweater with a big pocket in it so I could bring my statue of Saint Rita with me. I went to Saint Rita's grammar school and I was married at Saint Rita's Church. I always prayed to Saint Rita even when my husband was in the war. She brought me good luck. I didn't tell anybody that I had Saint Rita in my pocket. Number five has always been my lucky number, so I picked the fifth horse in the fifth race. I was the winner! I won $300,000 doled out over fifteen years. After Uncle Sam got his cut, it was about $14,000 a year. I was up on stage with Andy Williams getting the prize. He was really nice. He asked me what I was going to do with the money. I said, "I'll probably give some to the church." When I got home there were three priests waiting for me. I said, "Hey wait. I haven't gotten the check yet."

—*Marie A. Good, Our Lady of the Ridge parish, Chicago Ridge, Illinois*

One Sunday afternoon a priest was in the mental ward of a hospital giving comfort to the patients. One man approached him and said, "Glad to meet you, Father. I'm God."

The priest shook his hand and said, "Tell me, God, I was reading the bible the other day and I have a question about . . . "

The man put up his hand and stopped the priest. "Sorry, Father, but I don't like to talk shop on my day off."

It Pays to Advertise

As reported in the *Wall Street Journal*, the four-century-old Ursuline order of nuns has employed an advertising agency to create an ad campaign aimed at recruiting women to join their religious order.

"It must be done subtly. After all, a hard-sell campaign probably won't make someone sign up for a lifetime commitment to poverty, chastity, and obedience. We had to pull back, because we felt that when dealing with the soul of God, a snappy headline wouldn't be the answer to anybody's questions," says Sive/Young & Rubicam copywriter Melanie Marnich. "It's not like selling a cheeseburger."

A priest from San Francisco, a priest from New York, and a priest from Chicago are granted an interview with God. They all get to ask Him one question. The priest from San

Francisco asks, "God, there are times when nature, which you created, can be so cruel. Will there ever come a time when we have no more earthquakes in our city?"

"Yes," God answers, "but not in your lifetime."

Then the priest from New York has his turn. He asks, "God, will there ever come a time that my parishioners will be free from the threat of all the crime in the streets?"

"Yes," replies God, "but not in your lifetime."

Finally, it is time for the Chicago priest to ask his question. "God, will the Cubs ever win the World Series?"

"Yes," says God, "but not in MY lifetime."

What's in a Name?

When I was in school we didn't know any of the priests' first names. I think it was a sin to know their first names.

—Rick Kelleher, Sacred Heart parish, East Grand Forks, Minnesota

Robert is walking by Saint Rita's Church when the pastor spots him and says, "I know you didn't come to mass last Sunday so you could play golf."

Robert says, "Father, that's a lie! And I've got the fish to prove it."

Just Our Little Secret

Father Daley helped me get my first marriage annulled. It took about two years before I finally got it. Then I met Grace and we fell in love. Grace's mother wasn't too wild about me. We never told her that I had been married.

We got engaged and went through our pre-Cana instructions with Father Daley. The day of our wedding, during the mass, Father Daley was giving his sermon. He just happened to mention the fact that I had been married before and it didn't work out. Grace and I just about died. Grace's sister was the matron of honor; she turned all the way around on the altar to see how her mother was taking this shocking news. Our wedding had been videotaped. When we got home, Grace's mother took the tape and watched it three times. She wanted to make sure she had heard the priest right. Besides revealing our "little secret," Father Daley also made comments about our weight. I was a chef and Father said, "It's obvious that Kevin eats as much as he puts out for the customers. The bride, too, they could both stand to go to Weight Watchers."

—*Kevin and Gracemarie Good, Our Lady of the Ridge parish,*
Chicago Ridge, Illinois

A guy is weary of his hectic life. He decides to join a group of Trappist monks in a remote monastery high in the mountains. The monks are very strict; each monk is required to take a vow of silence. Once every ten years each monk meets with the friar in charge of the monastery and is allowed to speak three words.

Ten years pass, and the guy is called into the friar's chambers. "My son, do you have anything to say?" the friar asks.

The man nods his head and says, "Food's no good."

The old monk nods and notes it in an ancient leather-bound book.

Another ten years pass, and the elder friar summons the guy into his chambers once more. "You have been with us now for twenty years. Is there anything you would like to say on this occasion?"

"Bed's too hard," says the guy as he bows to the elder monk.

The monk nods and again takes out the tattered book and writes in it.

Finally, thirty years have passed; the guy is once more called into the friar's living quarters.

"Another decade has passed. What do you have to say?" asks the friar.

"I want out!" says the guy.

"Well, it's about time," says the monk. "You've done nothing but complain since you got here."

Non-Catholic Makes Contact with Archbishop

According to an article in the *National Catholic Reporter,* David W. Mueller, a distributor of the *Crusader,* an anti-Catholic comic book published in California, was arrested in Milwaukee, Wisconsin, for reportedly attacking Archbishop Rembert Weakland. Mueller was accused of hitting the archbishop in the mouth, back, and shoulders with a roll of contact paper. Several priests took chase after the attack but Mueller eluded them by spraying one priest with a squirt gun filled with an unidentified substance.

A nun is praying in the chapel: "Please, God, I pray to you morning, noon, and night and yet my life is nothing but misery. My students are unruly, I'm allergic to the food they serve in the convent, and even wearing this habit gives me a rash. But look at Sister Ann Joseph. She's always late for mass and she never gets up in the middle of the night to pray like I do. Yet she has well-behaved students and a happy life. Why am I, who obeys all the rules, being punished? Why, God, is Sister Ann Joseph, who never tows the line, being rewarded?"

A voice booms out: "Because Sister Ann Joseph isn't bugging me all the time—that's why."

Sister Tricky Dicky

Sister Marie Cajetan looked just like Richard Nixon.
—*Marcella Friel, St. Coleman's parish, Ardmore, Pennsylvania*

A priest checked into a high-rise hotel in downtown Manhattan. He noticed the window was open, and he was about to close it when he saw a man standing outside on the ledge. The priest leaned out the window and said, "Don't jump! Let me give you a hand."

The man said, "I don't want a hand."

"Then please let me call the police; maybe they can help."

"I don't want the police," said the man.

"Then, my son," said the priest, "let me administer the last rites."

"What the hell are last rites?" said the man.

"Go ahead and jump, you heathen!"

Keeping Track of the Priest with the Big Blue Eyes

I took instructions on Catholicism from the local priest who was about twenty-five and very, very handsome. Every Tuesday night I would go to the rectory and just he and I would sit in the big parlor. We'd talk about Catholicism but I was more interested in his big blue eyes. He was darling and so nice. I had the hots for him. Years later, friends still send me newspaper clippings about the priest because they knew I had a crush on him.

—*Judith A. Winters, Presbyterian, Freeport, Illinois*

A priest in Cleveland is having a rough year in his parish. The church building fund is not pulling in any money, more and more people are moving out of the parish, and his administrative assistant just quit. He goes to a psychiatrist and tells him his problems. The psychiatrist says, "You need a few days off. Take off your collar and let your hair down. Why don't you go someplace where nobody knows you?"

The priest buys a plane ticket to Miami. He takes off his collar and relaxes by the pool. That night he goes to a movie and enjoys a few glasses of wine before dinner. After dinner he's wandering down the street and finds himself in a topless nightclub. The bare-breasted waitress comes up to his table and says, "What can I get you, Father?" The priest is amazed and stutters, "How did you know I'm a priest?" The waitress says, "I'm Sister Margaret Mary. I go to the same psychiatrist."

Something of a Spiritual Nature No Doubt

One time I went to confession to Father O'Toole. Usually the confessional was very dark so you couldn't see the priest, but he had the light on. He needed light because he was reading a paperback novel. I never did get a look at the title.

—*Jack Kowal, St. Leo's parish, Chicago, Illinois*

During his sermon the priest was making an impassioned plea for more money for the church building fund. "We are asking that all parishioners donate one tenth of their annual income to the building fund."

One of the men in the front pew turned to his wife and said, "Let's not donate. Next thing you know they'll be asking for one twentieth."

Taking Out the Garbage in Latin

In the novitiate it was like living in a different century. Not quite the Middle Ages but more like the seventeenth century. We could only speak in Latin. Of course we had to make up Latin words for things like, "Take out the garbage." There is no Latin word for garbage. Garbage became *quisquillia*, meaning "whatever's in the can."

—*Anonymous Jesuit priest*

Invading the Convent

We went to see my aunt, a retired nun, at her mother house in Wisconsin. There were about five of us visiting. We knocked on the convent door and this old, old nun opened the door. She must have been ninety-five. "Good morning, Sister," we all said, "We are here for a visit." The old nun was very pleasant but definitely had gone off the deep end. She said, "Look in the sky, a milky white sky. On a day like this the invaders will come. They are coming because we are being punished for birth control. On a day like this they will come, it is written."

The invaders didn't come, at least not while we were there.

—*Peggy Regnier, St. Leo's parish, Chicago, Illinois*

A priest went hiking with a group from his parish. They got caught in a terrible thunderstorm. As they crouched in a shelter, one of the parishioners said, "Father, can't you do something?"

"Sorry," said the priest. "I'm in sales, not management."

Sister Mary Fido

I have a history of dressing like a nun. The first time I was in the second grade. The nuns let us come to school in our Halloween costume but not just any costume. We had to dress as our patron saint. My mother and I thought that there must be a million Saint Katherines. We figured if she was that holy she must have been a nun. My mother made me a little black and white habit.

The second time I was in my late twenties. My friend Lari, my husband, and I all dressed as nuns for Halloween. The lowest of the low was when my dog got a nun outfit. In Oakland, as a fundraiser, they had a pet parade with a costume theme. They had one category, "Pet and Owner Look-Alike Contest" and that's where my dog Lucy and I came in. My dog has always been Catholic so I dressed Lucy in a veil and I wore a matching black and white habit. We won first place.

—*Kathy McGilvery, St. Brendan's parish, San Francisco, California*

The Roaring Atheist

As reported in the *San Francisco Chronicle*, in 1962 Attorney Vincent Hallinan filed a suit against the Catholic Church claiming that the church unduly influenced David F. Supple to will $176,000 to the church with promises of heaven and threats of hell and purgatory. In the lawsuit Hallinan, a fallen-away Catholic who described himself as a "roaring atheist," challenged the church to prove the existence of these places.

What is black and white and black and white and black and white?
A nun falling down a flight of stairs.

Getting Off Easy

One Fourth of July, my little brother and cousin were playing with firecrackers in my uncle's backyard. The back of my uncle's property was right next to a Catholic church. One of the fireworks went through the open window of the church and caught the building on fire. The fire department was called. The church didn't burn down but the fire did cause substantial damage. My brother and cousin had to apologize to the priest. The priest was pretty easy on them. He didn't make them convert to Catholicism or anything.

—*Linda Kay Bristow, Methodist, Divernon, Illinois*

A wealthy man visits a small Catholic church for the first time and hears the priest deliver a very eloquent sermon. After mass the man shakes the priest's hand and says, "Father, that was one goddamn great sermon."

"Thank you," says the priest, "but it would be appreciated if you didn't use such language to express yourself."

"I just can't help it, Father. It was so goddamn good I wrote you a check for a thousand dollars."

The priest says, "No shit!"

13

THE VATICAN FOLLIES

Maybe it's the unusual modes of transportation (the Popemobile and a 747 named Shepherd One) or the commerical products made in his honor (Popecorn and Pope-on-a-rope soap). Whatever the reason, Catholics love to laugh about the shenanigans surrounding His Holiness.

The pope, the president, and the mayor of Chicago are in a lifeboat after their ship has sunk at sea. Provisions are running low and there is only enough left for one person to survive. Each must make his case to the others. First the mayor of Chicago pleads his case: "I am the mayor of the most powerful city in the world. We have Sears Tower—the tallest building—and we have O'Hare Airport—the largest airport in the world. The city will fall apart without me as the mayor." Next the president makes his case: "I am the president of the greatest country in the world. People in fifty states look to me for comfort and aid. The country cannot go on without my leadership." Then the pope talks: "I am the spiritual leader of Catholics from all over the world. I have to continue God's work on earth." They cannot decide who should live and so they decide to take a vote.

The president gets one vote, the pope gets one vote, and the mayor of Chicago gets 350 votes.

Dial-a-Pope

Global Telecom Ltd., a start-up in Ventura, California, this week began offering a 900-number phone service and said it will donate part of the revenue to the Vatican. Seekers of the holy word can dial 1-900-740-POPE and hear, in English, a tape of Pope John Paul II giving his daily message. The communique is transmitted to the service each day by Vatican Radio. . . .

The Vatican set up a similar line through the Italian phone company two years ago, but the service, in which callers use international phone lines, got off to a bad start and hasn't recovered. "The problem was, the pope spoke in such broken English that callers were turned off," says Mr. McEldowney, who sampled it.

—Wall Street Journal

As the pope is walking across the Vatican plaza, he spots a teenager leaning up against Saint Peter's and smoking a cigarette.

"Young man," says the pope, "please put that cigarette out."

"Screw you," says the punk to the pope.

"You dare to say such a thing to the pope! I am the pontiff, the holy father, the bishop of Christ, the most holy anointed of God, and you dare to say to me, 'Screw you'? No, my son, it is I that say to you, 'Screw you.' "

I Thought He Flew Coach

Dallas—Pope John Paul II will fly back to Rome after his U.S. visit aboard "Shepherd One," a plane equipped with a specially installed bed, American Airlines said yesterday.

The bed, between twin and full, will be covered by specially ordered Belgian linen sheets, embroidered pillow cases and a down comforter. It will be enclosed by a curtain.

Movie selections in the first-class cabin will include an

edited version of *A Few Good Men, Strictly Ballroom,* and *A League of Their Own.*

The dinner service will include caviar and a choice of roasted veal, beef tenderloin pignoli, chervil chicken or salmon with linguine.

Dessert will include ice cream sundaes with Godiva chocolates. The pope's only request was to have a cake on the flight.

—Reuters

Late one night at the Vatican, the pope is arguing with the devil. Satan claims no one on earth has a perfect memory. The pope says he knows an Indian in Arizona who never forgets anything. The argument becomes more heated until finally the pope agrees to give his soul to the devil if the Indian ever forgets anything.

The devil and the pope take a jet to Tucson, rent a jeep, and drive out to the desert to find the Indian. They see the old Indian sitting in front of his house. The devil says, "Do you like eggs?"

"Yes," answers the Indian.

Twenty years later the pope dies. The devil thinks, "Now's my chance to claim his soul." Satan goes down to earth and finds the old Indian. The devil raises his hand and says, "How."

The Indian says, "Scrambled."

The Pope Is a Sugar Fiend

As reported in the *San Francisco Chronicle,* American Airlines' flight attendant May Lannes was Pope John Paul II's personal flight attendant when he flew back to Rome from his trip to the United States in August 1993.

Lannes said the pope had a hearty appetite and takes his coffee with lots and lots of sugar.

Ever flown on Vatican Airlines? In case of an emergency the instructions are in Latin so the clergy can get off first.

Oh Those Golden Laces

An update on the tennis shoes with gold shoelaces sported by the pontiff on his trip to Colorado: The Pope sent assistants to Denver's Athlete's Foot shop, where they purchased a fifty-dollar pair of size 10 white leather shoes. They made one request: that the standard white laces be replaced with gold laces.

—Chicago Sun Times

The pope is visiting the United States on a whirlwind tour.

He's speaking at Madison Square Garden in New York and has to catch a plane to Chicago so he can address the faithful at a gathering in Wrigley Field. He gives his final blessing to the crowd, then rushes out into the traffic and hails a cab. The cab driver can't believe he's picked up the pope in midtown Manhattan. "Step on it, driver," says the pope. "I've got to catch a plane in twenty minutes."

"Your Holiness," says the awestruck driver, "it would take a miracle to get us out of this traffic jam."

"This is nothing compared to the traffic in Rome. If you don't mind, let me drive."

The pope jumps in the driver's seat and the cabbie gets in back. The Holy Father is racing through traffic, running red lights, and going the wrong way down one-way streets. Finally, a police car pulls him over.

The cop looks in the cab and is in a panic. He excuses himself and radios back to headquarters for instructions.

"Chief," says the cop, "you won't believe who I just pulled over for speeding."

"The mayor?" asks the police chief.

"More important than the mayor," says the cop.

"The governor?" tries the police chief.

"Much more important than the governor."

"You pulled over the president?"

"No, no, he's more important than the president."

"Who could be more important than the president of the United States?"

"I don't know his name, but the pope is his driver."

What's in a Name? The Official Titles of . . .

Nun—Sister or Mother

Priest—Father

Monsignor—Monsignor

Cardinal—Your Eminence

Archbishop and Bishop—Your Excellency

The Pope—His Holiness the Pope, Bishop of Rome and Vicar of Jesus Christ, Successor of Saint Peter, Prince of the Apostles, Supreme Pontiff of the Universal Church, Patriarch of the West, Primate of Italy, Archbishop and Metropolitan of the Roman Province, Sovereign of the State of the Vatican City

How to Get in Shape for the Pontiff

A San Pedro man whose white racing pigeons will be released at the Coliseum mass to symbolize doves of peace takes the birds out every evening for a short flight to get in shape.

—Los Angeles Times

A rabbi and a priest are having a friendly discussion about the merits of their religious commitments. The priest says, "Actually, as a priest I have more opportunity for advancement. I can become a bishop, a cardinal, and perhaps one day I could become pope."

The rabbi says, "And that's as far as you can go?"

The priest says, "What do you expect me to do after being elected pope, become God?"

The rabbi says, "Why not? One of our boys did."

Don't Give Up Your Day Job

As reported in *People*, a former menswear model and bossa nova singer, Daniel Serra, brags that he is the man who made a record with Pope John Paul II. Serra, a native of Brazil, convinced the Vatican to let him audiotape a homily the pope gave in Saint Peter's Basilica in 1983. Serra had original music composed and played under the pope's seven-and-a-half-minute sermon that he marketed as a 45-rpm disc. An original tune by Serra, "God Is Love," is on the B side of the record. Sales of the record were disappointing.

Pope for Sale

The pope doesn't get to the United States all that often, but when he does everyone is anxious to cash in on his pope-ularity. The following is a roundup from *People* and *Time* of unauthorized pope memorabilia:

Pope-shaped car air fresheners

Pope-on-a-rope soap

Pope-scopes (cardboard boxes fitted with reflectors that act as a periscope for seeing over crowds)

Pope masks—John Paul II's likeness complete with miter

Buttons featuring the pope in a Detroit Tigers cap with the phrase "Bless You Boys"

A lawn sprinkler shaped like the pope called "Let Us Spray"

Popecorn

Lip-shaped "Papal Pucker Ring" from Popepuree Co.
A rubber pope hat

A Hell of a Problem

The papal mass at Arizona State University's stadium Monday posed a devilish problem for church officials planning for the visit of Pope John Paul II.

The 75,000-seat facility is decorated with devils armed with pitchforks—the "Sun Devils" that are the university's mascot.

During the two-and-a-half-hour mass all the "Sparkies," as the devils are called, were covered with banners.

"Our goal is to create a prayer environment," Father Dale Fushek, who is in charge of arrangements, said before the event. "We can't hide the fact it's a football stadium, but we don't want to highlight it."

—Los Angeles Times

Frank and his friend Stan are out on the golf course when they run into Arnold Palmer. Stan says, "I know Arnold Palmer." As soon as Arnie spots Stan he walks over and shakes Stan's hand and they talk about old times.

"I can't believe you know Arnold Palmer," says Frank.

"Oh, that's nothing," says Stan. "I'm also a very close personal friend of Bill and Hillary Clinton."

"No way," says Frank.

"I'll show you," says Stan. He picks up the telephone in the clubhouse and calls the Clintons. The next thing you know, Air Force One has landed at a nearby airport and Stan and his friend are in Arkansas having dinner with the president. The president even asks Stan his advice about the economy. Frank can't believe that Stan knows the president.

"That's nothing," says Stan when they return home, "I am very close to the pope."

"His Holiness. It can't be true."

"I'll show you."

The two men fly to Rome and in no time are standing in Vatican Square. The pope is about to come out and give his blessing to the crowd when Stan disappears. A few minutes later the pope is standing on the balcony and Stan is right there beside him with his arm around the pope.

Frank can't believe his eyes. Before he can say anything, the man next to him says, "Excuse me, do you know who that guy standing next to Stan is?"

Did I Park the Popemobile in Reno or Rio?

According to an article in *Time,* the pope has twenty popemobiles at his disposal. Six of the bulletproof automobiles are kept in garages at the Vatican and the other fourteen are waiting for him in cities around the world. Most of the popemobiles—Renault, Peugeot, GM, Toyota, and Mercedes Benz—have been donated by the manufacturers.

Cutting the Rug

An enterprising Albuquerque man did not steal the rug from under the pope's feet during World Youth Day, but he did buy it.

And now for three dollars a square inch, you too can have a piece of the carpet where His Holiness is said to have trod.

Following the papal mass at Denver's Cherry Creek State Park on August 15, Dennis Bylina purchased 16 square yards of white carpet from Freeman Decorating Co., which supplied the carpeting upon which the pope walked. No one from the company was available for comment.

"Hurry before you miss this unique opportunity to posses a very unusual piece of religious history," reads Bylina's press release.

—*Religious News Service*

The Vatican Rag

Words and Music by Tom Lehrer

First you get down on your knees,— Fid-dle with your ro-sa-ries,—
So get down up-on your knees,— Fid-dle with your ro-sa-ries,—

Bow your head with great re-spect,— and gen-u-flect, gen-u-flect, gen-u-flect!
Bow your head with great re-spect,— and gen-u-flect, gen-u-flect, gen-u-flect!

Do what-ev-er steps you want, if You have cleared them with the Pon-tiff,
Make a cross on your ab-do-men, When in Rome— do like a Ro-man,

88 † WHAT'S SO FUNNY ABOUT BEING CATHOLIC?

Ev-'ry-bod-y say his own Ky-ri-e e-le-i-son, Do-in' the Vat-i-can
A-ve Ma-ri-a, Gee, it's good to see ya, Get-tin' ec-stat-ic an'

Rag. sort-a dra-mat-ic an' do-in' the Vat-i-can

Rag!

Get in line in that pro-ces-sion-al, Step in-to that

14

"DID YOU HAVE TO SHAVE YOUR HEAD?"

A Tell-All Interview with a Former Dominican Sister

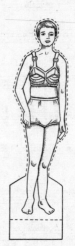

Daydreaming in Catholic school, I'd think about some of the greatest mysteries of our faith. What does Sister do for fun? How does she get all that stuff up her sleeve? Does she have to wear regulation nun underwear?

I was convinced the details of the personal habits of nuns would remain forever shrouded in mystery until I met a former Dominican sister and she agreed to an exclusive tell-all interview. We met for breakfast. Over scrambled eggs and coffee she answered all my questions. . . . I had a very long list. For reasons that will become obvious, she preferred to remain anonymous.

The Interview

Karen: Did you have to shave your head?

Sister X: We didn't when I was in but there was a time in the congregation when they did. I've heard the sisters talk about it. Before they took their temporary vows the sisters used to shave their heads. They would shave their heads a week or so before profession of the final vows. They would take a razor and get a butch haircut, take off all their hair. This custom actually started out in the monasteries as a way of preventing lice. Through the years it became spiritualized. They used to just cut the hair (not take it all off) as a way of renouncing the material world. The saints used to do it; Catherine of Sienna did it when she didn't want to be married off and so did Clare of Assisi. They used to cut their hair but they never shaved their heads. They cut it very short because in those days a woman with short hair couldn't marry. The shaving of the hair was actually a corruption of what the original purpose was—setting yourself aside for God.

Although there may have been some orders that continued to shave their heads, for the most part it was a onetime thing. Nuns kept their hair short because if you are wearing the coif (the tight piece of material that goes around the face and around the back) you get hot. For practical reasons, you wanted short hair. I know of one nun who was in the order for a very long time; her hair became very thin from wearing the veil all those years. When her order changed to wearing lay clothes she had practically no hair at all and had to buy a cheap wig. It wasn't a Dolly Parton wig but she looked almost that goofy.

Karen: Wasn't that coif you had to wear under the veil irritating?

Sister X: Most of the sisters got used to it but some sisters would break out in terrible rashes.

Karen: How did that veil hold together on your head?

Sister X: The veil is put together with Velcro; even the wire mesh frame under the veil is held together with Velcro. People are always shocked when they hear these ripping sounds when we take off the veil. We are so up-to-date.

Karen: Before Velcro how did they hold those veils together?

Sister X: It was put together with straight pins and safety pins. The great big veil (which the sisters used to wear) was attached to the coif; there was a forehead band which was just a heavily starched piece of material. In later years it was a piece of plastic that went around the head. The veil was put on top of this and fastened with three pins in a triangular fashion to secure the veil onto the head. It was quite a production getting dressed in the morning and they did it without mirrors because mirrors were a sign of vanity. It wasn't until Vatican II that the sisters could have mirrors.

Karen: What was your habit like?

Sister X: I was in the convent after Vatican II so mine was the modified habit. It had four parts: a slip, the tunic that was just an A-line dress, the scapular over the tunic, and the veil.

Karen: Your habit was pure white. How did you keep it clean?

Sister X: In the novitiate, we were issued one habit a week, so we had to be very careful not to get it dirty. Our tunic didn't have pockets; the pocket was in the slip. There was a slit in the dress and you could reach into the slit and pull something out of the pocket in your slip. Very practical for keeping your dress clean. Also in the old days the scapular part of the habit always looked very well pressed. What the sisters used to do was take the scapular and fold it very neatly at the end of the day and place it under their mattress at night.

Karen: Did you have summer habits and winter habits?

Sister X: We would wear the same habit all year. In the winter I used to wear long underwear underneath. I was getting ready for mass one morning at 6:00 A.M. and I am not a morning person. I was putting on my veil and I looked in the mirror and my long underwear was hanging out. I had put on my long underwear, I put on my slip, I put on my scapular, but I had forgotten to put on my dress. When I looked in the mirror I realized my mistake. I am thankful I was a post-Vatican II sister and was able to use a mirror or I would have gone into mass in my long underwear and scapular.

Then there were the long rosary beads tied around the waist. I've heard stories about a sister who would be really angry with a kid and she'd whip around really quickly and say, "Oh, I caught you with my rosary. I'm so sorry, dear."

Karen: Let's get personal. Where would you buy your underwear?

Sister X: They used to have sisters' catalogues. One was called "Fitzpatricks"—a good Catholic name. It was a sisters' supply store. They had different kinds of habits you could order. They also had a selection of underwear—basic styles, all white, cotton. I used to buy mine at J. C. Penney—all white.

Karen: Do nuns wear bras? I mean you can't tell what's under there anyway so what's the point?

Sister X: Yes, they do. Actually, it depends on the era a nun entered the convent; if bras were commonly worn in society when a woman enters the convent she'd wear a bra.

Karen: Ever wear Fredricks of Hollywood underwear?

Sister X: Who would care? And our clothes all went to a common laundry with our laundry number sewed on. Can you imagine the laundress looking at a sexy bra and saying, "465 is getting wild."

Karen: When I was in school I used to marvel at all the things the nuns pulled out of their sleeves: rosary beads, handkerchiefs, bibles, rulers. How do you get all that stuff to stay in there?

Sister X: My habit was more like a dress so we used the pocket in our slip rather than our sleeve. The only thing I can say is there must have been pockets. I do know that the sisters who had very long sleeves used to wear stitzels, which were fake sleeves. They would roll up their sleeves above the elbow and put on the stitzel and they *would stay on with old-fashioned elastic bands like garters. This relates to keeping your habit clean because you had to wear it for a week. They could wash out the stitzels during the week.*

Karen: *You were a teaching sister. Were there sisters in your order who did things like the cleaning and the cooking?*

Sister X: *Some orders actually had so-called lay sisters who were like a rank below the teaching nuns. There was a pecking order. The lay sisters would do all the grunt work. In some cloistered communities there are extern sisters, sisters who could go out of the community and do the shopping, run the errands, and get the things they need for the inside. They would also greet people at the door. These sisters are considered a rank below.*

In my congregation we had sisters in Germany during the world wars. In Bavaria, in some cases, the young women were sent to the convent because the family couldn't afford to feed another child or couldn't afford to marry off their daughter. But who knows how God works? Possibly these women really did have a vocation but because they were peasants and weren't educated they did the farming, the cleaning, and the cooking. One problem the congregation is having now is that the sisters who did that kind of work are dying out and they don't have sisters who want to do the domestic chores. There was a mentality among the domestic sisters that they weren't as good as the teaching sisters.

Karen: *After teaching all day what would you do after you came home besides correct arithmetic papers? What was a fun night in the convent?*

Sister X: *We always looked forward to Friday nights because that's when they brought out the beer. It was Lucky beer because that was the cheapest brand; we had a very stringent budget. Simple things made us happy, like a bottle of cheap beer. We would also celebrate a sister's patron saint's day. We'd have parties for that and put on skits.*

Karen: *You put on skits? Tell me about that.*

Sister X: *Usually the skits would satirize the religious life. I remember one in particular called the "History of the Apron." One sister went to the beach and she dared to pull up her sleeve just above* *her wrists and took off her shoes and socks and pulled her habit just above her ankles. That was her idea of sunbathing.*

Karen: *Relaxing in the convent, would you have to wear the full habit?*

Sister X: *It depends on the congregation. In my case, yes, we would wear the habit in the convent. You just get used to it. My sister and I were going to Disneyland and we stayed at a convent in L.A., cheaper than a hotel. She was scandalized when we were in the common room watching TV and the sisters wandered in wearing their pajamas.*

Karen: *You can watch TV?*

Sister X: *Oh yes, even in cloistered orders the sisters get the newspapers to stay in touch with the world. The theory is that nuns have to pray for the world and how can they pray for the world if they don't know what's going on. You are removed from worldly things but you don't totally dismiss the world.*

Karen: *Do sisters get to take a summer vacation?*

Sister X: *We had a one-week retreat each year and we could take a one-week home visit. Sisters who lived a long distance would go home once every three years and that had to do with expense. Our congregation owned property in the mountains; the sisters had built cabins there. There was another property at the beach so we could go there.*

Karen: *The beach? What would you wear?*

Sister X: *Our habit. We'd take off our shoes and socks and get our toes wet. It was torture. Before I left, the congregation had loosened up a lot and we could wear bathing suits. In fact, I remember, I was teaching near the beach and sometimes after school I would ride my bike down to the beach in my shorts and bathing suit. I was walking down the beach in my bathing suit, a modest one-piece but a bathing suit nonetheless. I was in my early twenties and I was in pretty good shape. I spotted one of my students with his dad. He was yelling, "Sister, Sister, Sister," totally oblivious to the fact that I was wearing a bathing suit. His father on the other hand just about dropped his teeth. He was speechless.*

Karen: Is life in the convent very regimented?

Sister X: Somewhat. We had prayers at 5:30, dinner at 6:00, night prayer was at 7:00 or 7:30, morning prayer and mass together. It was important to our community to have prayer together.

Karen: How many other sisters were in your community?

Sister X: Our congregation had a rule we couldn't have fewer than four in our house. One year I lived with just four sisters and another year I lived with thirty-four. The number of sisters in the convent depended on the size of the school and who else was living there like the superintendent of schools.

Karen: Did each sister have her own room?

Sister X: Yes, we each had our own rooms and we could have what we wanted in them. Each room had a bed and a desk. How many ways can you rearrange your room with a bed and a desk in a little square room? There were maybe two different configurations. There was a sink and a medicine cabinet in each room. Showers were down the hall.

Karen: Since you had a private room, could you stay up until 4 A.M. reading?

Sister X: Oh sure. But in the novitiate it was like boot camp, lights out at ten o'clock! They were shaping us for religious life.

Nineteen seventy-six was the first year that they allowed women into the armed service academies. A very good friend of mine was accepted to the Air Force Academy. We used to compare notes. We had lots of common experiences—ever try finding black shoes in the middle of summer? Sleeping late was 6:30, and we would both read with a flashlight under the covers after lights out.

Karen: Did many of the women drop out in the boot camp phase?

Sister X: That's when most of them drop out. My group, we had twelve. About eight made it to profession and there are four or five that are still there—less than 50 percent.

Karen: When Christmas rolls around it's always a dilemma to figure out what to buy a nun. What would people give you?

Sister X: Stationery, gloves, handkerchiefs, scented soaps were the stock gifts. The sisters used to joke about it. People don't realize that part of taking the vow of poverty is being detached from things. Most of the gifts we got we would turn in and give to the superior because things were held in common. If there was something that we wanted to keep we would ask permission.

Karen: Do you remember a gift that you had asked to keep?

Sister X: Let's see. One year my mother gave me a bathrobe that had to be dry-cleaned only. Not very practical in a convent. She bought it at Bullocks so I asked permission to take the bathrobe and exchange it for a pair of shoes. I really needed shoes.

Karen: If you did need a pair of shoes or new underwear how did you get the money to pay for it?

Sister X: We would go to our superior and ask if we could buy it. Next, we would see the treasurer and say that we had permission to buy a pair of shoes. She would give us a check, cash, or the credit card.

Karen: The credit card? You had a credit card?

Sister X: The congregation had a credit card for either J. C. Penney or Sears; nothing high-end like Macys.

Karen: What about gifts? Could you buy gifts?

Sister X: We could get permission to buy very simple gifts.

Karen: Would you exchange gifts in the convent?

Sister X: Yes, usually we would make homemade gifts. Holy cards were a popular gift. They would be pen and ink drawings or pressed flowers. Clear contact paper was the big thing in my congregation; it was like laminating it without a laminator. We would contact paper the holy cards or make bible covers or write sayings in calligraphy or make collages.

Karen: What gift recommendations do you have for a civilian to buy a nun?

Sister X: Don't give scented soaps because most sisters don't use them. We used to give them away by the bushel. It depends on the sister. Now that I think about it, a nice bottle of wine.

Karen: Wine? Are you kidding?

Sister X: I am serious. Contrary to popular belief, sisters do drink wine. On Christmas and special occasions we appreciated a good bottle of wine with our meal. Something the whole congregation can enjoy. Another example of a good gift might be a CD. I have a friend who listens to all kinds of music. Most convents have CD players and tape recorders. Or a book that a sister might particularly want. If you feel comfortable, ask her what she would like as a gift. I know one sister who is a marathon runner. She would have loved a pair of running shoes.

Karen: Do nuns still practice self-mortification? Or did that go out with the Middle Ages?

Sister X: There are sisters who still fast and some still use "The Discipline." "The Discipline" was essentially a rope that had knots tied in the end like a little whip. You would hold it in the front and whip it so it would hit you in the back. In the Middle Ages some saints whipped themselves to bloodying themselves, which is really an abuse of it. It is used with the examination of conscience as self-mortification.

Karen: Where would you get this whip?

Sister X: It was given to you when you professed. A couple of nights a week before they went to bed the sisters would use it.

Karen: Did you use it?

Sister X: No, no, no. They used them up until Vatican II.

Karen: Any other forms of mortification?

Sister X: Some sisters would get up in the middle of the night to pray. One sister had a particular devotion to her patron saint. Each night she would get out of bed at 2 A.M. and pray to the saint. But one night she opted to stay in bed and the saint's picture fell off the wall. She said, "I got up really fast."

I've been on retreat and gotten up in the middle of the night to pray. It's a really beautiful time to pray.

Karen: Can you tell me about relics? How did it happen that we venerate a piece of a saint's toe?

Sister X: *It's always interesting to explain this to kids because they are grossed out. There are first-class, second-class, and third-class relics. The first-class relic is a piece of the bone, the skin, or the hair of the dear departed. A second-class relic could be a piece of clothing that they wore. A third-class relic is anything that they touched. There is a store in the Vatican where you can buy bone fragments and other relics. They are sealed with wax into a little case the size of a quarter and you get a certificate of authenticity stating that this is Saint So and So's finger bone. To us it sounds weird but think of it in terms of the age in which these holy men and women lived. They didn't have anything like personal possessions. You know when your mom dies you want her favorite comb or her watch. Back then there were no photographs and nothing to remember them by. The people lived very poorly. To have a "piece" of them was an object of veneration. It was a different culture. And we still carry on the tradition today.*

Karen: *Without giving away your identity, I am curious how sisters are named.*

Sister X: *Some orders use names like Sister Jane Doe. I know Sister Nancy's, which I think sounds really goofy. In my order they would never have given me my real name. The tradition is from the Old Testament; when God gives you a calling you take on a new name. Which is why popes change their names. I took the name from the Old Testament of a very strong woman who stood up to men. We submitted three names that we wanted. Usually the first name was the one you were given. We used to joke about names like Sister Mary Moses of the Burning Bush. It is interesting that priests are known by their last name and nuns go by their first name.*

Karen: *Did you interact with the priests at your parish?*

Sister X: *Some priests you didn't want to interact with! It would really depend on the individual priests. Some want to have the "good sister" relationship. "Oh, the sweet good sisters," with the priest playing God. That didn't usually work out too well. Sisters had to grit their teeth and smile and take it in order to maintain relations in the parish.*

Karen: Are you saying that some priests are male chauvinists?

Sister X: There is a great deal of chauvinism. Today's sisters are very bright, and very articulate. They are not going to put up with this garbage anymore.

Karen: Somehow I had the idea that the nuns interacted with the parish priests. That you took care of the altar clothes.

Sister X: Some do. What's really funny is that pre-Vatican II the only way a woman could stand on the altar was to clean it! She could go there and vacuum and dust and wax but boy don't go up there for any other purpose. In the United States "equal rites" is a big issue for many sisters.

Karen: In conclusion, any thoughts about the pope?

Sister X: Things would be a lot better if only His Holiness wasn't as afraid of American women as American women are supposed to be of him.

15

IT'S A MIRACLE

Changing water into wine, the Shroud of Turin, the appearances of Our Lady at Lourdes are just a few of the "official" church miracles. But any Catholic can tell you miracles happen every day: not getting caught rolling your uniform skirt up above the knees; a refund check from the IRS; or the traffic cop letting you off with just a warning. These things are truly miraculous!

Father Francis Shaughnessy was noted for his uncanny ability to always make the wrong decision. If he had a choice of elevators, it was the one he chose that would stall between floors. If he went to the racetrack, the horse he bet on would come in last. If he planned the annual parish picnic, on the day he picked there would be a thunderstorm.

Father Shaughnessy had to fly out of town on important parish business. When he made his reservation, much to his relief there was only one airline that flew to his destination. There was no decision to be made! Feeling confident, he purchased his ticket and got on the plane.

Halfway through the flight the pilot announced that the plane's engines had quit working and the plane was about to crash in the ocean.

Father Shaughnessy started praying to his patron, Saint Francis. He prayed, "Please, Saint Francis, in my entire life I've never been able to make the right decision. Whenever there is a choice to be made, I always make the wrong one.

But on this flight I thought I was safe. There was no choice to be made. Why am I being punished this way?"

As soon as Father Shaughnessy finished his plea, a giant hand came out of the clouds and lifted him out of the plane. He was suspended in the heavens while the plane crashed down to the ocean.

A heavenly voice said, "My son, I have saved you because you have called upon me."

"Yes," said the priest, "I have called on you, Saint Francis."

"Er," said the voice, "would that be Francis Xavier or Francis of Assisi?"

The Miracle Roses

Growing up, Mrs. Gonzalez was our neighbor down the street. She had dug up her whole yard and enshrined Mary in a bathtub. She had the most incredible roses surrounding the shrine. Mrs. Gonzalez swore it was Mary's influence that made her flowers so beautiful. Her Bathtub Mary roses were the envy of the neighborhood. Much later we discovered that her husband would go fishing and clean the fish in the basement. At dawn he'd bury the fish guts in her grotto rose garden.

—*Mitchel A. Robuck, St. John Cancius' parish, East Chicago, Indiana*

The Scooting Nun

One of the nuns at Mother McAuley High School was an invalid. She'd ride around the hallways on this scooter. No one had ever seen her out of the scooter. One day she was scooting through the halls when she spotted a mouse. She hopped up and squashed the mouse with her foot, got back on the scooter, and drove off.

—*Christine Kowal, Christ the King parish, Chicago, Illinois*

George is in France and comes up with a scam for smuggling French wine into the United States without paying any duty. He dresses like a priest and has hundreds of bottles of wine labeled with a picture of a cross. As George is going through customs, the agent says to him, "What's in the bottles?"

"Why, holy water from Lourdes."

The agent opens one of the bottles, smells the contents, and says, "This isn't water, it's wine."

"Saints be praised, it's another miracle."

Miracle Nuns Help Dateless Office Workers

One of the places I shop for unusual Catholic gifts—glow-in-the-dark Madonnas, plastic domed saints, and altar boy awards—is through the Archie McPhee catalogue. My favorite Archie McPhee item is the bag-of-nuns. The 2¼-inch sisters fit over the tips of your fingers and make great finger puppets. I was so taken with the tiny nuns I called the folks at Archie McPhee's in Seattle to ask about the popularity of the plastic sisters.

Aimee Macdonald of Archie McPhee's claims she receives hundreds of letters attesting to miracles that the nuns have performed. The following testimonial will prove her point:

Dear Archie McPhee,

My last order included a bag-of-nuns. The office I work at is full of spinsters. If one of my co-workers is a righteous woman of high integrity that hasn't had a date in a long time, she is asked to become a member of the Nun Club. Members of the Nun Club proudly display their nuns taped to the top of their cubicle walls.

Since I brought the nuns, I became the first Mother Superior. One of my first edicts was that the first member getting a date had to remove her nun and relinquish her membership in the club. One quiet afternoon, I heard a commotion near my wall. My nun had sprung her Scotch tape pedestal and projectiled into the hall. (I wouldn't lie. I was Mother Superior.) Shortly after that, I did get a date and had to give up my religious office.

I didn't know if this was a religious experience or a sign, but it did indeed occur. We haven't told too many people about this because we don't have time for visiting pilgrims. Mother Teresa has since become Mother Superior and keeps her eye on all of us fallen nuns.

Please be careful who you sell the bag-of-nuns to, avoiding religious zealots or nasty people who might take advantage of these nuns' powers to get dates.

Thanks, Archie, for improving my social life.

        —C.J.F., Peoria, Illinois

The Message from Fatima

While it hadn't occurred to me that you might be the font of knowledge from which this might flow, it did occur to my best friend. The mystery surrounds the message the Blessed Virgin left to the children in Fatima, Portugal. It was to be opened some fifty years later, but curiosity got the better of the pope and it was opened before the time elapsed. The message was never revealed. What's the secret? Was it that horrible? Do you think the National Enquirer *might know?*

        —M.R., Washington, D.C.

Before loosing my mighty torrent of knowledge, M., I'll have to provide a little background for those teeming millions who never learned the charming story of Fatima because they were wasting their formative years having impure thoughts and eating hamburger on Fridays. You might do well to pay attention yourself, because your letter contains a couple of regrettable misconceptions.

Though the Catholic Church is naturally reluctant to recognize tales of miracles, cures, apparitions, and the like, it has deemed credible the story of the Blessed Virgin's appearances at Fatima to three Portuguese children: Lucia dos Santos, age ten, and her cousins Francisco and Jacinta Marto, nine and seven. After the first of these appearances—they occurred monthly from May through October of 1917—word got around that something neat was going on, and with each sub-sequent visit increasing numbers of people came to Fatima to have a look. Only the children could see and hear the Lady, however; the rest had to be content with a moving cloud, a rustling cloud, and on the final visit a grand miracle, wit-nessed by 100,000 people, in which the sun danced around the sky for ten minutes.

Among other things, the Lady allegedly told the children that World War I would end soon, that another great war was coming, and that two of the children, Francisco and Jacinta, would be taken to heaven shortly. They died of influenza within three years. The third child, Lucia, entered the convent in 1925. Though the Lady of Fatima had told the children to keep certain of their conversations secret, Lucia eventually succumbed to pressure from her religious superiors and set down the three-part "Secret of Fatima" in various written memoranda beginning in 1941. The first two parts, which Lucia revealed relatively freely, were quickly made public: (1) The Lady of Fatima showed the children a vision of hell, including demons that "could be distinguished by their terri-fying and repellent likeness to frightful and unknown ani-mals." (2) In order to prevent "war, famine, and persecutions of the church and of the Holy Father," the Lady said she would return to ask for the "Consecration of Russia to my Immaculate Heart."

Lucia wrote down the third part of the secret, much more reluctantly, after Christmas of 1943, and it is this part that remains a mystery. Her memoir was sealed in an envelope and given to the bishop of Leiria, Portugal, to whom Lucia expressed her wish—not, as far as anyone has been able to determine, the Lady of Fatima's wish—that it remain sealed at least until 1960, when it would definitely be opened and made public. Before the year of truth arrived, however, the docu-ment was passed to Rome, under circumstances that do not shine very clearly through the mist of history. Pope Pius XII, who died in 1958, may have read it, and Pope John XXIII and a few cronies certainly did, probably in 1959. John said, "This makes no reference to my time"; though Lucia was still alive, he dispatched the document to the archives and left the matter to his successors, none of whom has yet seen it fit to come clean.

The papal cover-up, combined with the red-baiting, fire-and-brimstone nature of the revealed parts of the secret, has led many observers to speculate that the message is one of nuclear apocalypse. I, however, have it on good authority that it was a personal missive to Pope John. To wit:

Dear Jack,

What's all this about birth control? We never said anything about birth control. Please check your files and advise ASAP.

Regards, G.

P.S.: Kennedy for President!

—*From* The Straight Dope *by Cecil Adams*

A couple of nuns were driving in the country when they ran out of gas. The only container in the car was a chamber pot that their young students used on picnics.

The nuns took the pot and walked to a nearby farmhouse. The farmer was happy to help and filled the chamber pot to the top. The nuns returned to the car and were carefully pouring the gas into the tank. A passenger in a passing car said to his wife, "Wow, that's what I call faith!"

The Apparition Treasure Map

We associate miraculous appearances with faraway places like Lourdes or Fatima. But in recent years reports of apparitions of Mary and Jesus here at home seem to outnumber Elvis sightings. Here's a useful guide to unusual and unscheduled appearances of Our Blessed Mother and her Son.

*Hurricane Gloria swept through Milford, Connecticut, in 1985. Besides more serious damage, the winds from the storm tore a

branch from a maple tree. As reported in an article from the Associated Press, the owner of the tree noticed that the resulting knot in the tree resembled the face of Jesus.

*The New York Post reported that in an apartment building in Manhattan the image of Jesus appeared between a double pane of glass in Rosa Diez's fifth-floor bathroom window. Police had to set up barricades to control the crowds.

*According to Time, a woman in Stone Mountain, Georgia, claimed that she saw the face of Jesus in a forkful of spaghetti that was displayed on a billboard.

*An article in Time revealed that Rita Ratchen saw an image of Jesus on a soybean-oil storage tank while driving near her hometown of Fostoria, Ohio. The amazed Rita is quoted as saying, "I see it as a natural phenomenon. . . . It is caused by the lights and the rust . . . but I believe the Lord permitted it to happen."

*Arlene Gardner of Estill Springs, Tennessee, claims to have seen the face of Jesus on her General Electric freezer on the front porch of her mobile home. Not everyone in the town was impressed with the heavenly vision. People reports that Mayor John Gaul, of Estill Springs, said, "If Jesus were coming to this town, he would have come somewhere different than on a damn freezer."

*At Saint John of God's parish in Chicago a wood carving of the Virgin Mary, Rosa Mystica, was said to weep. As reported in the Chicago Tribune, in July of 1984, when the statue failed to produce any more tears, a Ronald O'Neil took a pistol and shot the dry-eyed virgin. The carving didn't bleed.

*Progresso, Texas: "Hundreds of people a day have visited an auto parts store to view what they believe is the Virgin Mary's image on a bathroom floor.

"The image—varying shades of gray that store owner Reynaldo Trevino said were once one color—appeared December 3 on the cement floor of the shower stall in the rear of his Progresso Auto Supply."

—San Francisco Chronicle

*Lake Arthur, New Mexico: "Maria Rubio was rolling a burrito for her husband's dinner one day last fall when she noticed that the skillet burns on the tortilla resembled the mournful face of Jesus Christ crowned with a wreath of thorns. . . . Father Joyce Finnigan, a missionary who reluctantly blessed the images, insists that Mrs. Rubio's 'Jesus on the Tortilla" is just another kitchen accident."

—Newsweek

*In South Phoenix, Arizona, a picture of Our Lady of Guadalupe painted by Estela Ruiz's husband has been speaking to Estela since 1988. As reported in the tabloid Our Lady Queen of Peace, Pittsburgh Center for Peace, Mrs. Ruiz asserts the first words she heard from Our Lady were "Good Morning, Daughter."

16

BINGO AT QUEEN OF MARTYRS, EVERGREEN PARK, ILLINOIS

Bingo and Catholics go together like Holy and Ghost. Eager to expand my knowledge of this religious form of recreation, I did a little field research. Everything I wanted to know was explained to me during Bingo night at Queen of Martyrs. The volunteer staff were happy to share their experience about the most popular of Catholic pastimes.

The Big Picture

Everyone working here is a volunteer. Normally we have three volunteers working back here. There are always latecomers buying cards at the last minute. We get here early and set up in the room in the back. At the start of the night I get a bank from the rectory; we need cash so the Bingo card sellers can make change. At the end of the evening we give our bank back to the rectory. We have to make sure we have $2,250 to pay the winners. The slowest night I ever had was a profit of $150. The biggest night was over two grand. From what I understand the profits are used for the upkeep of the school.

The Bingo cards cost all different amounts. You have to have a door card—they're a dollar. We have a game called the Lucky 14. The Lucky 14 card costs a dollar. If you have Bingo with a Lucky 14 card you win $200. But if you have Bingo without the Lucky 14 card then it's only worth $100. They then keep playing until someone with the Lucky 14 card hits Bingo and that winner gets the other $100. We have two $500 prizes: one for the tenth game and one for the nineteenth game. The fourth game is worth a $100 payoff. The rest of the games pay $40 or $80 depending on which cards you have; regular cards pay $40 and the bonus cards are worth double that amount. We play twenty games in all.

The most difficult patrons to satisfy are the hard-core players. They play Bingo numerous times a week at different parishes and clubs. From them, there are always suggestions on how we should handle our games. Since no one person wanted to be singled out to handle complaints, we formed a committee of four. This way it's four against one. Ninety percent of the Bingo players are not from Queen of Martyrs parish. We have no idea how many are Catholics.

—*Pat Melloni, Bingo cashier*

Old Balls . . . New Balls

One of the regulars told me one time that we had old balls and we should buy new balls. The numbers she wanted weren't coming up. I told her, "The balls are $65 a set. There's nothing wrong with these balls." But she kept insisting there was something wrong with the balls. We had a $500 game and guess who won? The woman who was complaining. I went up to her after the game and said, "Now that you won the $500, how about contributing $65 to buy new balls!" She just looked at me.

—*John Sylvester, Bingo caller*

Selling Lucky 14 Cards

I volunteer to sell the Bingo cards. I have three other girls working with me. First we wash down all the tables, then I get a bite to eat on the run. After that I settle in and sell the Lucky 14 cards. I save tables for some of the players too. I'm a jack-of-all-trades. We have real friendly people here, real friendly. If you are new to the game and you come back to play, the people will help you out.

The regular players come early and spread out their cards and put out their good-luck charms, troll dolls, pictures of their family, Saint Jude statues, even elephants. Some of them come here three hours early to play Bingo. The get their cards and tape them together; some people have twenty or thirty cards for each game. They always complain they don't win, but I know better. Some of these people go from place to place playing; they even go to Indiana. They have pots of $250 and $1,000 at a Serbian church in Cherryville.

When I sell the cards I lay out the Lucky 14 cards and people come and look them over. They are looking for their lucky numbers, certain inside numbers and certain outside numbers. I don't have a system; it's just mere luck. Who knows what they are going to call? After I sell the tickets, I relax and have fun and play. I've been playing Bingo umpteen years. It wasn't even legal to play when I started playing. I won $500 a couple of years ago and I put the money aside. I use that money to play. I keep track by marking my calendar with how much I spend. I still have some of the Bingo winnings left.

—*Geri M. Boelcke, Lucky 14 card seller*

Keeping the Peace

I work security on Thursdays. This is an easy detail; we don't have many problems with the Bingo players. Some of the players get here very early. You have to be fast. It is supposed to take only twenty-eight seconds between numbers.

Besides keeping the peace, my job is to take the fellow who handles the money to the bank. The law in the State of Illinois is that you can only have winnings up to $2,250. It used to be $3,200 but the state changed it. I never get involved with how much profit the church makes from the games; that's not my concern.

—*Matt Schleder, Bingo security guard*

17

THINGS THEY NEVER TOLD US

While the priests, sisters, and brothers filled our heads with vast amounts of knowledge, some subjects were strictly taboo.

The Legend of the First Female Pope

It is whispered about in monasteries and convents, hinted at in scholarly church circles. Was there a female pope? Is she the greatest cover-up in church history?

The stories of Pope Joan, aka John Anglicus, first started circulating about the year 1250. In the publication *Universal Chronicle of Metz* (attributed to Dominican Jean de Mailly) it was first stated that a woman, disguised as a man, had worked her way up in the curia as a notary and managed to become a cardinal. She was preceded by Victor III as pope. The brilliant and talented popess's sex went undetected until one day she was mounting a horse and she gave birth to a child. Not only was the vow of celibacy broken but (gasp) . . . a woman pontiff! The attending faithful did the only Christian thing; they tied Joan to the horse's tail, dragged her around the city, and then stoned her to death.

Joan's papacy was given much credibility during the Middle Ages. Don't forget in those days they didn't have soap operas and cheap tabloids to feed the collective imagination. Gradually the gossip about Pope Joan became embellished with sordid details. After giving birth and being killed by the outraged citizens, she was buried on the spot where the shameful episode took place. This narrow street, the story goes, was avoided by her papal successors. But not all the tales about Joan were negative. One advanced thinker, Mario Equicola of Alvito, used the example of Pope Joan to demonstrate the equality of women—an idea that has yet to catch on in Rome.

Priests Have to Cook and Clean

Eight Jesuit priests live here in a community. Four of us cook and four of us clean. I cook. I'm a pretty good cook. It's all part of bachelor survival. For me cooking is more of an adventure than drudgery and I don't have to cook three meals a day. Usually it's one meal in the evening and the rest you are on your own. I also do the grocery shopping, I shop at Lucky.

—*Anonymous Jesuit Priest*

A new arrival in heaven was walking around when she ran into the Virgin Mary. The woman was so happy to see the Blessed Mother she didn't know what to say. The Virgin Mary invited the woman to join her for tea. The woman said, "Blessed Mother, it must have been so wonderful being the mother of the Lord. How did it feel being the mother of Our Savior?"

The Virgin Mary said, "To be honest, Joseph and I were hoping he would have been a doctor."

It Was All a Bunch of . . .

My first day at Saint Mary's University, in theology class, the priest walked up to the podium and asked, "How many of you have been to Catholic schools?" We all raised our hands. Father said, "Everything you've learned is bullshit." I went, "Ahhhhhhh."

—*Coleen Martin, Christ the King parish, Chicago, Illinois*

The Church Has Miracle Busters

In an article in *USA Today*, Father James Gil, one of the Catholic Church's miracle investigators, is quoted as saying, "I've never seen evidence that I thought was convincing.... Miracles do happen, but rarely."

Catholics Borrowed Traditions from Pagans

The hot cross buns that you eat on Good Friday follow the English custom of bread bearing the sign of Our Lord's cross. Actually, the tradition of bread with a cross dates back to the Saxon pagan era. The symbol represented the goddess Oester.

Best Way to Choose a Priest for Confession

There were different types of priests for confession. One type of priest, no matter what you said—if you lied to your mother or stole or whatever—would give you a penance that was unbelievable. This type of priest had nobody lined up in front of his confessional. He'd be outside smoking a cigarette.

But another type of priest would have a line a mile long. He is what we called the "Three and Three Priest." Even if you committed murder, that priest would give you a penance of three Hail Mary's and three Our Father's.

—*Jim Breheney, St. Gabriel's parish, Stamford, Connecticut*

18

KEEPING TRACK

Catholics have many things to keep track of: How many weeks since our last confession? How many days will our suffering in purgatory be reduced if we say the rosary? Is the annunciation a holy day of obligation? How many angels will fit on the head of a pin? . . . You get the idea.

But Where Do You Cash Them In?

The nuns used to tell us how much time in purgatory each of our sins was worth. I'd tally up my sins and see how many indulgences I had to offset my suffering in purgatory. I always thought of indulgences as green stamps.

—*William Callahan, St. Aidan's parish,*
Jersey City, New Jersey

Racing Pagans

At our school the students would have pagan baby races. In the front of the classroom the nuns had a fund-raising chart with cutouts of the pagan babies. Little pagan babies stacked on top of each other. It was similar to those thermometers charities used to measure how much money was collected. For each dollar we contributed the nun would put a pagan baby on the chart.

—*Annette Sandoval, Our Lady of the Pillar's parish,*
Santa Ana, California

They Aren't?

The neighborhood I grew up in was Mexican, so I thought everyone in the world was Catholic.

—*Daniel Hernandez, Holy Family parish, San Antonio, Texas*

Getting the Most for Your Money

I thought, "A quarter for one votive candle? No way." I'd drop a quarter in and light the whole row.

—*Jonathan Yorba, Saint Martha's parish, La Puente, California*

I Bet This Guy Works for the Government

In high school, Brother Billingham—who was at least a hundred and ten years old—used to collect money for missions. He didn't have one of those round tin cans; he would collect the money in his open hand. Every day the guy who sat in the first seat would say, "Brother, I have a quarter but I only want to give a nickel." So after making the rounds Brother Billingham would give the guy twenty cents change. Every day it was the same scenario: "Brother, I have a quarter but I only want to give a nickel." And Brother would give him twenty cents change. The first day back after Christmas vacation, Brother Billingham took up the collection but this time the guy didn't have his usual quarter to contribute; he gave nothing. After collecting from the rest of the class, out of routine Brother Billingham gave the kid twenty cents change. For the rest of the year the guy got twenty cents from the senile Brother Billingham.

—*Jack Kowal, St. Leo's parish, Chicago, Illinois*

The High Cost of Smoking

At my high school we used to get demerits. Five demerits and you got a detention. Chewing gum or eating was two demerits plus a two-dollar fine. When you got five demerits you had to come to school on Saturday and clean the school.

Our school was located way out in the boondocks; it took forty minutes just to get there. You could buy off the demerits for five bucks. The big one was getting caught smoking—twenty-five demerits and a twenty-five-dollar fine.

—*Madelyn Johnson, Our Lady of the Ridge parish, Chicago Ridge, Illinois*

On Your Mark, Get Set, Go

I'd collect rosary beads. I had all sizes: some for small purses and some for big purses. I'd race and see how fast I could say the rosary. HailMaryfullofgracetheLordiswiththee . . . "

—*Margaret Komet Hensley, Saints Simon and Jude parish,*
Brooklyn, New York

19

CATHOLICS GO TO THE MOVIES

When we choose a Catholic form of recreation a good movie ranks right up there with Bingo and the church bazaar. Maybe it's because Hollywood has made so many films about Catholics: religious epics (King of Kings), musicals (Jesus Christ Superstar), biographical films (Mother Teresa), movies with a moral (I Confess), lighthearted comedies (Nuns on the Run), and even horror movies (The Omen).

The Legion of Decency

Class A, Section I—Morally Unobjectionable for General Patronage

Class A, Section II—Morally Unobjectionable for Adults and Adolescents

Class A, Section III—Morally Unobjectionable for Adults

Class A, Section IV—Morally Unobjectionable for Adults with Some Reservations

Class B—Morally Objectionable in Part for All

Class C—Condemned

In 1934, a Chicago Jesuit, Father Daniel A. Lord, published an analysis of 133 feature-length films. From these humble beginnings was born a powerful arm of the Catholic Church: the Legion of Decency (LOD). During its more than forty-five-year reign, the Legion of Decency developed a formalized movie rating system. The movie ratings would appear weekly in local Catholic newspapers. A quick check of the ratings ruined more than one Saturday afternoon's entertainment for the truly vigilant movie fan.

Film buffs may want to test their knowledge of movies' ratings by filling out the LOD Crossword Puzzle.

THE LEGION OF DECENCY CROSSWORD PUZZLE

Puzzle created by Alberta Fox, St. Patricia's parish, Hickory Hills, Illinois
(answer key appears on page 128)

Across

3. The Greatest ———— On Earth. *It's a B rating for suggestive costumes under the Big Top.*

5. *Initials of a two-word phrase meaning baloney; if used in a movie the LOD would find it morally objectionable.*

8. ———— to Macon County. *Condemned for being too violent, too sexy, and too pointless.*

11. *Michael* ———— *starred in* Alfie, *the AIV modern-day morality play.*

13. *The Sabbath? Not! Condemned? Yes!*

15. *Rated AII East of* ————. *Paradise?*

16. ——— Mules for Sister Sara. *In this AIV film prostitute Shirley MacLaine poses as a nun.*

17. *The AII* Brother Sun, Sister Moon *showed the saintly life of Francis of Assisi, who loved animals and wrote* ————.

18. *AI* Two Years Before the ———— *featured Barry Fitzgerald who played the crusty older priest in AI* Going My Way.

19. *What you might call the halo of* Saint Joan. *Rated AII (the movie, not the saint).*

23. *An AI for* ———— the World in 80 Days *and recommended in "A Choice Collection of Family Movies" by the U.S. Catholic Conference.*

26. ———— Baby. *A sacrilegious thriller, witches, and the anti-Christ equal a condemned rating.*

28. *Joseph was Jesus'* ——, *not his Ma, in* King of Kings. *Rated AIV because the filmmakers used too much poetic license retelling the story of Christ's life.*

29. *Because* Frankenstein's Daughter *was born here and not under God's law the LOD gave this a B rating.*

30. The Moon —— Blue *was condemned because of the careless use of the word "virgin."*

33. *In AIII* Bunny ———— *aging bank robbers make a career of breaking the seventh commandment.*

35. —— Dog Coll *received a B rating for violence, brutality, sadism, and indecencies.*

36. The ———— in Needle Park *received the LOD rating C for too much graphic sex and too many illegal drugs.*

38. ———— of Boys Town. *The AII sequel to the AI* Boys Town, *which brought the life of Father Flanagan to the Silver Screen.*

39. ———— Window. *An AII hit for Catholic director Alfred Hitchcock.*

41. —— Doll *was condemned from the pulpit by Cardinal Spellman of New York—ditto for the Legion of Decency.*

42. *Billboards for movies of all ratings.*

44. *In* ——— Stop, *Marilyn Monroe's sexy rendition of "That Old Black Magic" contributed to the B rating.*

45. ——— Lobo. *A typical John Wayne film with lots of violence and a little sex, an AIII.*

46. To Be ——— Not to Be. *The title of this AII World War II comedy refers to Shakespeare, not the sin of taking one's life.*

47. *If Father O'Malley of the AI* Going My Way *had been a Protestant minister he would have received this degree (initials) from the seminary.*

48. *Think of the LOD ratings as a* ————— *from which to choose an A-rated movie.*

49. —— Were Strangers *and we are not going to see this B-rated John Houston film.*

50. *AI for* The Greatest ——— —— ———. *John Wayne had a cameo appearance as a centurion at Christ's crucifixion.*

Down

1. ——— MacMurray *starred in the AI* The Miracle of the Bells.

2. *AI for* Ben-———, *the "Tale of Christ." The book by Lew Wallace was blessed by Pope Leo XII.*

3. The ————— of Kilimanjaro *was based on a story by Catholic convert Ernest Hemingway. Rated B for justifying immoral actions.*

4. *For reasons clear only to network executives, the AI-rated* The Wizard of ——— *airs on televison during Easter week.*

5. *What Italians do when they censor a condemned filmo.*

6. *The AIII rated* West ——— Story *featured hit song "Maria."*

7. *The AI* ————— of the Kingdom *starred Gregory Peck as a Catholic missionary.*

9. *In this movie Adam's wife had* Three Faces *and a B rating.*

10. *The AI* The —— Commandments *had the best special effects miracle in movies—the parting of the Red Sea.*

11. *Another name for the AII* The Silver Chalice. *A Hollywood version of the making of the chalice used at the Last Supper.*

12. *Brando's sexy performance in* A Streetcar ——— Desire *contributed to the movie's B rating.*

13. *Setting for* The Front Page. *The 1974 remake's profanity earned the movie an AIII rating.*

14. *B for a suggestive sequence in* —— *as a Stranger.*

16. *Scarlett's home in* Gone With the Wind. *One reason it received a B rating—Rhett Butler used the word* damn.

18. The —————————— *of the Wedding, an AII rating for this ceremony.*

20. "Heigh- ————," *a song featured in the Disney classic with the snow white AI rating.*

21. *I Escaped from Devil's* —————. *Too much sex and too much blood for the LOD, a Condemned.*

22. Don't Go ———— the Water *and don't see this B film with suggestive dialogue and situations.*

23. Play It —— It Lays. *An AIV rating for the double S—sex and suicide.*

24. What's ————, Tiger Lily. *The LOD found this Woody Allen film smutty, tasteless, and Condemned.*

25. Mary Poppins' *AI profession.*

27 The Best ————— of Our Lives. *Rated B because at the conclusion the movie implied divorce and remarriage.*

31. *The B-rated* For Whom the Bell Tolls *was set in this country.*

32. ————— Stiff. *Don't be scared to see this AI Lewis and Martin comedy.*

34. Act of the —————. *Genevieve Bujold loves priest Donald Sutherland in this AIV movie.*

35. Harold and ——————————. *This AIII film depicted the forbidden sin of suicide.*

37. All ——— Eve. *It's a "B" for Anne Baxter's nonbiblical Eve.*

40. ————— Tide. *AII film featuring Catholic character actor Barry Fitzgerald.*

41. ——— Rabbit. *An AI animal from Disney's* Song of the South.

43. *The AII* To ——— With Love *starred Sidney Poitier of* Lilies of the Field *fame.*

46. The ———— and the Pussycat. *A B for prostitute Barbra Streisand repeatedly breaking the sixth commandment.*
48. Somebody Up There Likes ————. *The AII life story of Catholic boxer Rocky Graziano.*

Something for Catholic Couch Potatoes: A Collection of Movies Available on Home Video

Boys' Town (1938)
Spencer Tracy, Mickey Rooney

An automatic plenary indulgence for renting this Catholic video classic. Before there were boyz n the hood there were boys in the town. In his most saintly performance Spencer (Father Flanagan) Tracy builds a home for juvenile delinquents. Tough guy Mickey Rooney tests the limits of Spencer's philosophy: "There is no such thing as a bad boy." He ain't heavy, Father. He won an Academy Award.

The Cardinal (1963)
Tom Tryon, John Huston

This is the story of an Irish-American priest who gets a membership to that exclusive all-male club the College of Cardinals. You know how some priests' sermons just seem to last forever? Tryon captures that feeling of eternity on celluloid. . . . *The Cardinal* goes on and on and on.

Change of Habit (1969)
Elvis Presley, Mary Tyler Moore

What would Mr. Grant say? Actually, Mary Tyler Moore as a nun is an inspired bit of casting. "Sister" Mary must choose between the King—Elvis Presley—and the King of Kings—Our Lord. No contest. Be sure you "offer up" the boredom you are sure to suffer watching this tedious Elvis drama.

Going My Way *(1944)*
Bing Crosby, Barry Fitzgerald

Father O'Malley (Crosby) wins the hearts of his crusty (but lovable) superior and the respect of the rowdy (but lovable) neighborhood gang. Because of his performance in this classic many consider Bing Crosby worthy of canonization. Sainthood is doubtful but the film was blessed with Academy Awards for actors Crosby and Fitzgerald and an Oscar for best song "Swinging on a Star."

I Confess *(1953)*
Montgomery Clift, Anne Baxter

Father Montgomery Clift hears the confession of a murderer and later is unjustly accused of committing the crime himself—the kind of dilemma that students ask about in theology class. True to form, Catholic film director Alfred Hitchcock adds lots of suspense to the sacrament.

The Last Temptation of Christ *(1988)*
Willem Dafoe, Harvey Keitel, and Barbara Hershey

Director (and former seminarian) Martin Scorsese's controversial film based on Nikos Kazantzakis's book. The human Christ has doubts about his role as Our Savior. Recommended for viewing by highly spiritually evolved Catholics only. All others must promise to fast forward through Mary Magdalen's (Barbara Hershey's) marathon sex scene. Proceed with caution—your intentions must be pure.

Lilies of the Field *(1963)*
Sidney Poitier, Lilia Skala

Sidney Poitier helps to build a chapel for a group of feisty but charming German-speaking nuns and wins an Oscar for his efforts. The kind of movie you could watch with your grandmother or your sister if she happens to be a sister.

Mother Teresa (1986)
Narrated by Richard Attenborough

A documentary about everybody's favorite nun. The Nobel Prize–winning sister is seen traveling around the world from Africa to the Bronx. She's the only person you can term "a living saint" and be right on target. The kind of production that makes you proud to be a Catholic. Invite a non-Catholic over to watch this sure-to-win-converts film.

Sister Act (1992)
Whoopi Goldberg, Maggie Smith, Harvey Keitel

Motown meets Mother Cabrini. Whoopi—a Vegas lounge singer on the lam from her Mafia boyfriend—gets things shaking as the convent's new choir director. In this film everybody wins: Whoopi discovers she looks good in a habit and the nuns discover rock and roll. Whoopi is just too much fun! You'll get your reward on earth watching this spirited film.

The Song of Bernadette (1943)
Jennifer Jones, William Eythe, Charles Bickford

A Holy-wood version of the story of the nineteenth-century French saint, Bernadette of Lourdes. Looking like they both just stepped off a holy card, Jennifer Jones plays Bernadette and Linda Darnell is the Virgin Mary. Keep a big box of Kleenex handy when watching this Catholic film classic.

We're No Angels (1989)
Robert DeNiro, Sean Penn, Demi Moore

Two ex-cons, DeNiro and Penn, escape from prison. To avoid the law they masquerade as priests at the shrine of the Weeping Virgin. In the end, bad boy Penn—Madonna's ex-husband—is won over by a life of prayer, fasting, and (can it be true?) chastity. The movie has a miracle (the little deaf girl can hear!) and spotlights religious conversion (DeNiro and Moore become converts).

That's Just Your Opinion

Catholics in films are great! Any time you deal with guilt and lots of sexual repression you get a lot of humorous material for films.

—*Jan Wahl, movie critic, KRON-TV, San Francisco*

20

FOOTBALL IS A CATHOLIC GAME

More than any other sport, football is a reflection of our faith: Games are won on a "Hail Mary pass"; a historic play is dubbed the "Immaculate Reception"; and through "Devine" intervention a Catholic football hero realizes his dream.

The Hail Mary Pass

The NFL divisional play-off game between the Minnesota Vikings and the Dallas Cowboys on December 28, 1975, is best remembered by Catholic (and non-Catholic) football fans for the "Hail Mary pass."

With eleven rookies on the Dallas team, 1975 was considered a rebuilding year and yet the Cowboys were able to secure a wild card berth in the play-offs. Veteran quarterback Roger Staubach (Roger-the-Dodger) led the Cowboys to victory that day at Metropolitan Stadium in Bloomington, Minnesota.

Late in the fourth quarter Dallas was losing to Minnesota 14 to 10. With 37 seconds left in the game, Staubach had the ball on the 50-yard line. He took the ball from the shotgun and waited as long as he could before throwing downfield to wide receiver Drew Pearson. Pearson grabbed the ball on the 5-yard line and lunged into the end zone. Final score 17–14 Dallas!

After the game a reporter asked Staubach what he was thinking when he made the miraculous pass. "I just closed my eyes and said a Hail Mary," said Staubach, a graduate of Saint John's grammar school in Cincinnati. "It just seemed natural. I guess it was all those rosaries I said growing up."

Roger Staubach claims that many of his Baptist friends in Dallas asked him, "Why didn't you call it the 'Hail Jesus pass'?"

It's an Unsolved Mystery of Faith

One of the most memorable (and possibly the most controversial) plays in NFL history was the Pittsburgh Steelers' "Immaculate Reception." On December 23, 1972, Franco Harris caught a last-second 60-yard touchdown pass thrown by quarterback Terry Bradshaw to beat the Oakland Raiders. Harris took possession of the football when it deflected off Raiders' defensive back Jack Tatum. The unresolved mystery is whether Steelers' running back John Fuqua touched the ball and tipped it to Harris. The success of this miraculous play put the Steelers in their first play-off in the team's then-forty-year history.

Myron Cope, the color commentator for the Pittsburgh Steelers, is noted for dubbing the play the "Immaculate Reception" but he takes no credit for creating the name for the play. After the game, Myron had dinner with his wife, then sat down to write his commentary for that night's news show. Just as he was putting the finishing touches on the story his phone rang. A woman from an advertising agency called and suggested that he call the play the "Immaculate Reception." Myron enthusiastically agreed that that was the perfect name for the play and used it on the eleven o'clock news. Myron scribbled down the name of the woman caller and the name of the advertising agency where she worked and kept the information for years. Unfortunately, he has lost track of the woman's name. Myron freely admits that it would be just another NFL play if it weren't for the inspired name "Immaculate Reception."

"Devine" Intervention

At 175 pounds, the 5'6½" Dan "Rudy" Reuttiger was an unlikely Notre Dame football hero. But in 1975, after defeating Georgia Tech, his Fighting Irish teammates (including the then unknown Joe Montana), carried Rudy on their shoulders into the locker room. This was the only time in Notre Dame history a football player was so honored.

Rudy first saw Notre Dame's campus in 1966 during his senior year in high school. From that day on he had a dream. That dream was to wear the blue and gold and play football for the Fighting Irish. His 1.7 grade-point average at Joliet Catholic made him barely eligible for his high school sheepskin, let alone a chance at tossing the pigskin at the country's top football college.

After a stint in Vietnam he was working a dreary job as a turbine operator. One of his friends was killed on the job. It was his friend's death that made Rudy realize that life is short and he should try for his dream. By the sheer force of his will Rudy was finally accepted at Notre Dame. The pudgy twenty-five-year-old junior pestered Coach Ara Parseghian into letting him try out for the team. Late in the season Parseghian left and Rudy had to try out all over again for Coach Dan Devine. Rudy made the team!

It was the last game of the season, Notre Dame vs. Georgia Tech. NCAA rules allow only sixty players to dress for home games. Rudy's name was not on the roster. Rudy was ready to quit in disgust. What he didn't know was that many of the other ND players had offered to give up their spot to let Rudy have his moment of glory.

The clock was winding down. The last minute in the game, the 59,000 fans in the sold-out stadium started chanting, "Rudy, Rudy, Rudy ... " Coach Dan Devine put him in the game as defensive end. Rudy sacked the quarterback; the crowd and team went crazy. This moment in football history may never have happened if it weren't for the coach's "Devine" intervention.

21

SCAPULARS, VESTMENTS, AND GREEN PLAID JUMPERS

In addition to all the normal things that non-Catholics wear, Catholics have a large assortment of jewelry, clothing, and other wearing apparel made just for them: green plaid jumpers, salt-and-pepper corduroy pants, cloth scapulars, and modest wedding gowns. When it comes to fashion, Catholics lead the way . . . silently and in single file.

The Spring Fashion Show

I took sewing lessons in my junior year of high school from Sister Mary Janis. Modesty in dress was the overall theme at the all-girl Mercy High School and it was especially stressed in sewing class.

The focus of that semester's work was on creating an outfit to wear at the school's annual spring fashion show. Naturally, since we had to display our handiwork to the entire school body, we put a lot of thought into choosing just the right fabric and pattern for our homemade dresses.

Sister Mary Janis guided us every step of the way. At the beginning of the school year she lined us up—we were always lining up for something—and with the precision of a drill sergeant she measured each of us. Sister wrote down exactly what size we were to buy from the selection of Simplicity patterns offered at Franks Department Store. I was amazed to discover that my pattern size was two sizes larger than my normal size 8. Being a good Catholic girl it never occurred to me to question Sister about this discrepancy. I just accepted on faith that patterns were sized differently from store-bought clothes.

After months of cutting, stitching, basting, and hemming, the day of the big fashion show arrived. About a hundred of us in Sister Mary Janis's multitude of sewing classes were ready to strut our stuff. One by one, we walked down the runway in the school assembly hall trying our best to make a fashion statement. We made a statement all right! Unfortunately, the message our fashions were conveying was something like, "I just graduated from Weight Watchers and these are my fat clothes." Our dresses just hung on us, revealing not a hint of a womanly curve.

Sister Mary Janis was pleased. This had to be the most modest display in the history of women's fashion.

—*Donna Swift, Saint Etheldreda's parish, Chicago, Illinois*

The Well-Dressed Bride

In recent years there has been a trend in the style of bridal attire which is frankly indecent and scandalous. It is difficult to establish precise standards in these matters, but the mature Catholic girl has an instinctive knowledge of what is in good taste. Too often she hesitates to follow her own better judgment for fear that she will be criticized for being out of style. If she will stop for a moment to consider the sacredness of the nuptial ceremony, the privileged position that the bridal party occupies at the altar, the fact that our Blessed Lord Himself is to be the Wedding Guest in Holy Communion, then she will understand how necessary it is that anything suggestive of the indecent be utterly excluded. She insists that her attendants also be dressed in good taste.

—*From* What Catholic Girls Should Know About Marriage *by*
Francis X. Dietz

A guy goes into business for himself and opens a dry-cleaning store. He decides to do an aggressive marketing campaign and goes door to door in the neighborhood soliciting new business. He knocks on the door of the Convent of the Most Sacred Heart. A nun answers the door and says, "Can I help you?"

"Yes, you can, Sister," says the dry cleaner. "I was just wondering if you had any dirty habits I could help you with?"

Love Your Hat

We couldn't walk into church without something on our heads. We had chapel veils, pieces of lace that we kept in little plastic rain hat containers. The old Polish ladies would have Kleenex bobby pinned to their heads.

—*Joan Each Rowan, St. Bride's parish, Chicago, Illinois*

Keeping the Wrinkles at Bay

We had the Dominican nuns in the full white outfits. This really old nun used to get hot and she'd undo the back of her headgear and her face would just fall out . . . all these wrinkles.

—*Coleen Martin, Our Lady of Lourdes parish, Decatur, Illinois*

Beating the System

We weren't allowed to wear sleeveless gowns for our sixth-grade graduation. About 60 percent or 70 percent of the class brought sleeveless gowns and wore shawls so the nuns couldn't say anything.

—*C. Kimberly Regan, Holy Spirit parish, Stamford, Connecticut*

Good Question

When my little sister was learning to talk, my parents took her to church. Right in the middle of the homily her little voice rang out over the congregation, "Mommy, why do priests wear dresses?"

—*Agnes Consolacion, St. Mary's Cathedral, San Francisco, California*

So That's Why You Wear Hawaiian Shirts

If I wear the Roman collar no one sees my face. I become a walking Rorschach test.

—*Anonymous Jesuit Priest*

The Way It Was

We wore middy blouses with a big red sash—not a little red sash—a big red sash tied with two equal-size streamers. The collars on the blouses had to be starched to the point that they made a sound if you touched them. I don't remember the nuns conducting starch checks but wilted collars were not acceptable.

—*Margaret Komet Hensley, Saints Simon and Jude parish,*
Brooklyn, New York

What Is Under There?

I had Sister Alberta in the first and second grade. I realize now that she was young but then I couldn't tell—she seemed ageless. I loved it when she walked because her little black boots used to pop out in front of her habit. I used to want to trip her just to see her legs. Was she real under there? Once in a while she would sit on the desk and you could see laces and ankles.

—*Daniel Hernandez, Holy Family parish, San Antonio, Texas*

Purity Protection for Only a Dime

An original essay by Will Dunne, St. Mary's, Chicago, Illinois
Will Dunne is a San Francisco playwright and author of such award-winning works as The Bridge, I Married a Werewolf, Eleventh Hour, *and* Mr. Smith Goes to Hell.

In a certain Dominican high school for boys in the Chicago area, purity protection was always within arm's reach Monday through Friday just outside the school chapel. At ten cents, the price was a bargain, even back then—the early 1960s—especially when you consider the alternatives of everlasting damnation, torment, and pain.

It all started about eight hundred years earlier when the young man who was to become Saint Dominic announced to his parents that he wanted to be a priest. Mater and Pater weren't too pleased with the news. In fact, they responded to it by locking Dominic up in a tower and threatening to keep him there until he changed his mind.

By the way, this is how I remember the story, which, even if I do recall it correctly about thirty years later, may not have been accurate in the first place. It's what the brothers—that is, the Dominican friars—told us.

Anyway, Dominic's parents thought that the least their son could do was to become a rich doctor or lawyer. Dominic, however, thought otherwise. He had been in Catholic school long enough to know that the fourth commandment (Honor thy father and thy mother) didn't apply if what they wanted you to do wasn't Catholic. And what could be less Catholic than not becoming a priest?

So Dominic stayed in the tower, praying for the enlightenment of his parents and for the dawning of a distant future in which one day he would have a religious order and several high schools named after him. Meanwhile, to Dominic's parents, the situation seemed hopeless. The kid wasn't coming out of his room.

Then they had an idea.

If Dominic could but once partake of the sweet pleasures of secular life—in other words, if only he could get laid—he would be out of that tower in a second and on his way to fame and fortune. So they put aside their own Catholic dogma for a moment and hired a prostitute to go up into the tower and do him.

By the way, this story is based on the assumption that nobody in his right mind could possibly resist a prostitute late at night in a lonely tower.

The plan was perfect in every way, except one: Dominic's parents overlooked the possibility that an angel could intercede and warn Dominic that impure thoughts, words, and deeds were just around the corner. And, ironically, that is exactly what happened.

The rest is history. When the prostitute arrived, she was greeted by a young man who was mysteriously able to resist each and every one of her sexual advances.

Exactly what these advances were is generally unknown, since the brothers never discussed the details of this part of the story. However, Dominic's secret was well broadcast: Just before the prostitute arrived, he knotted up a rope with a certain number of knots—the number had something to do with the rosary and might have been fifteen—and tied it secretly around his waist as tight as he could so that, all the while the prostitute was trying to seduce him, Dominic was in excruciating pain. Consequently, he was unable to respond.

Granted, another person under the same circumstances might have found the fifteen knots even more exciting than whatever it was the prostitute was doing but, in the world of my high school, this possibility was never even remotely considered.

So the prostitute left, her mission unfulfilled, and Dominic's parents were so impressed with his fierce strength of will and saintly determination—they didn't know about the secret rope trick—that they let him out of the tower and, with their blessing, sent him off to pursue his true vocation, which he did.

To some degree, the knotted rope has remained a symbol of purity among Dominican friars here and there over the centuries, but perhaps nowhere so much as at my high school just outside the chapel in 1960. It was there that, in memory of Saint Dominic, one could find a stack of "purity cords" lying like a limp shaft of harvested wheat over a black coin box near the chapel entrance.

Rather than gristly medieval rope, the friars used fresh white household string and, instead of pulling it torturously tight around your bloodied waist, you only had to wear it like a loose belt under your clothing. Nevertheless, the function and purpose were the same: With your purity cord on, you had protection.

Paying for your purity cord was always on the honor system which, considering the product, seemed more than appropriate. The cords were almost always available, except during spring when the supply tended to run out faster than usual. To obtain your purity cord, you simply put ten cents into the box and took the one that seemed to be calling your name. Then you went somewhere private and put it on.

Part of the purity cord's power, practically speaking, was that, after you had taken a few showers while wearing it, you could no longer untie the thing, or quickly slip out of it, no matter how hard you tried. Removing it required premeditation and a sharp knife.

Thus, even if you were to find yourself in what was known as an "occasion of sin"—for example, making out with somebody in the back of a car—you would be strongly inclined not to remove any articles of clothing within the vicinity of your waist for fear of exposing the knotty secret underneath. Result: *purity protection*.

And even if you did go so far as to somehow reveal your middle, you would then have the problem of explaining what that odd-looking, grungy string was doing there, by which time the reason you started to take your clothes off would be only a passing memory. Result: *purity protection*.

Actually, for a skinny Catholic high school freshman with large glasses and pimples, sexual situations—especially ones that involved the removal of clothing—weren't the type of occasion of sin that you had to worry about all that often. In fact, the purity cord's true purpose was to protect you from what was defined in the classroom as the sin of Onan and referred to in the locker room as whacking off.

The bottom line was this, pure and simple: With your purity cord in place, you could never really get naked. It was always there, day and night, no matter what you were doing or thinking about doing. Like a lasso from above, it had you caught in its grip, a heavenly reminder of how much Saint Dominic had suffered just for you.

22

FEASTING AND FASTING: EAT, DRINK, AND BE WARY!

When it comes to food and drink, Holy Mother Church has a heavenly menu for every occasion. At daily mass religious Catholics enjoy communion wafers and sacramental wine. Modern abstaining Catholics can feast on microwavable Mrs. Paul's Fish Sticks. Catholics with a chill take comfort in a bottle of Christian Brother's brandy. Irreverent kid Catholics love to munch on "cheese and crackers that got all muddy."

Good Food, Good Drink, Good God, Let's Eat

Just about every Catholic can recite the words to Grace before meals: "Bless us, O Lord, and these thy gifts, which we are about to receive from Thy bounty, through Christ Our Lord. Amen."

Do you know the words to Grace after meals? "We give Thee thanks for all Thy benefits, O Almighty God, who livest and reignest forever. Amen."

According to *The New Saint Joseph Baltimore Catechism*, you receive 300 days' indulgence for saying Grace after meals and zippo for Grace before meals.

A missionary is being chased through the jungle by a huge lion. The missionary is cornered by the man-eating beast and drops to his knees and starts to pray. He looks up and to his delight he sees the lion bowed in prayer as well. He says, "Thank you, lion, for joining me in prayer. I thought . . . "

"Don't interrupt," growls the lion, "I am saying grace."

My Mom's Recipe for Tuna Crappe

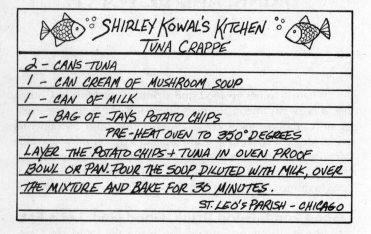

SHIRLEY KOWAL'S KITCHEN
TUNA CRAPPE

2 - CANS TUNA
1 - CAN CREAM OF MUSHROOM SOUP
1 - CAN OF MILK
1 - BAG OF JAYS POTATO CHIPS
PRE-HEAT OVEN TO 350° DEGREES
LAYER THE POTATO CHIPS + TUNA IN OVEN PROOF
BOWL OR PAN. POUR THE SOUP, DILUTED WITH MILK, OVER
THE MIXTURE AND BAKE FOR 30 MINUTES.
ST. LEO'S PARISH - CHICAGO

On Friday nights we always had tuna casserole made with salty potato chips. Noted for her sense of humor, my mother dubbed the concoction "Tuna Crappe."

—*The author*

Days to Avoid Roast Beef

Abstain from meat on Ash Wednesday, the Fridays of Lent, and Good Friday. The law forbids the use of meat, but not eggs, the products of milk or condiments made of animal fat. Permissible are soup flavored with meat, meat gravy, and sauces.

—*From the* 1993 Catholic Almanac

A Maryknoll missionary working in Borneo is captured by a tribe of cannibals. They tie the priest to a stake, nick him with their spears, and drink his blood. This goes on for several days until the holy man can stand it no longer. He pleads with the chief, "Please let me die, I beg you. I'm tired of being stuck for the drinks."

No Drumsticks for Capitalist Catholics

In my Baltimore catechism they had a picture of communists in their home eating a big turkey dinner. Outside the home, looking in the plate-glass window, was a starving Catholic family.

—*Peter Kowal, St. Leo's parish, Chicago, Illinois*

Another Use for Communion Wafers

On First Friday before mass began, you put the unconsecrated host into the chalice if you intended to receive holy communion. That way there were no leftover wafers. I used to swipe a whole handful of hosts and take them out into the parking lot. I'd spread peanut butter on the wafers and make communion canapes. It was okay because the hosts weren't consecrated.

—*William Callahan, St. Aidan's parish,*
Jersey City, New Jersey

A beer salesman from Germany goes to the Vatican and has an audience with the pope. He says, "Your Holiness, I am from Beck Beer. If you would change the words in the Our Father from 'Give us this day our daily bread' to 'Give us this day our daily brew,' we'd be willing to contribute ten million deutschmarks to the church."

The Holy Father scratches his head, then turns to his assistant and says, "Cardinal, when does our contract with Wonder Bread expire?"

No Thanks, I'll Have the Holy Water

Wade Davenport flashes from Denver that in anticipation of the pope's visit, a bar is featuring a coffee and brandy drink called Onward Christian Folgers, which is, yes, pretty desperate.

—*Herb Caen's column*, San Francisco Chronicle

God Will Protect You

As reported in the *Annals of Internal Medicine*, two Kentucky doctors, Terrance Furlow and Mark Dougherty, concluded that churchgoers who drink wine from a common chalice may be exposing themselves to several types of bacteria and the herpes simplex virus.

The First Catholic Deodorant

In Ireland, Tansy Pudding was served at Eastertime to celebrate the end of Lent. Tansy is a bitter plant with yellow flowers and a very strong flavor. Reputedly, tansy pudding is supposed to cleanse the body of bad odors after forty days of a smelly fish diet.

How do you make holy water? Take a pan of water and boil the hell out of it!

Something Is Mighty Fishy About This

My Catholic friend, Brenda, told me that the communion wafer tasted like the thin white sheets of fish food that used to come in a box. We'd have pretend communion and use pieces of the fish food as the host.

—*Patricia Duff, Protestant, Denver, Colorado*

Eat the Burger, Go Straight to Hell

I ate a cheeseburger at Mel's Drive-In at five minutes to midnight on a Friday night. I figured it was close enough to Saturday morning that it didn't make any difference. Just to be sure, I confessed my "sin." I went to a hard-core priest who has worked in a prison and told him about the cheeseburger incident. He said, "Son, do you think in God's eyes it makes a difference if it was five to twelve or ten to twelve or some other time on Friday? In God's eyes it's a mortal sin and you could be headed straight to hell!" Think of all the things he had seen and heard. How terrible was eating a cheeseburger on Friday compared to murder?

—*Anonymous, St. Gabriel's, San Francisco, California*

Two nuns were in a restaurant looking at the menu. Sister Anne said to the waiter, "I'll have a New York steak cooked medium rare."

"Excuse me, Sister," said the waiter, "this is Good Friday."

"Thank you. I was confused; I'll have a cheese sandwich."

Sister Rose looked up from her menu and said to the waiter, "Is it still Good Friday?"

How Do You Say Budweiser in French?

Our high school was coeducational—boys and girls in class together. This was practically unheard of in Chicago. We were taught by the Sisters of Saint Joseph. The sisters could not control the boys. One nun could not keep sixteen-year-old Bill Costello from drinking beer in the back of French class. Right after lunch, he'd be back there opening the beer cans— *swosh.*

—*Betty Czekala, Little Flower parish, Chicago, Illinois*

Oops

I remember when the mass was in Latin, this priest was consecrating the host. He bowed over and said the words and then he was supposed to elevate the host. Well he just stayed bowed over and his deacon was whispering, "Elevate the host, . . . elevate the host." And he said, "I can't. I just ate it."

—*Anonymous Jesuit Priest*

It's four o'clock in the morning in the Cloister of the Most Sacred Heart. Suddenly all the nuns are awakened by the clanging of the abbey bells. Alarmed, the sisters put on their robes and run to the main meeting hall. There stands Sister Mary Magdala with her arms folded. "Sisters," she says, "I have just received a very disturbing phone call. The caller would not identify himself, but it seems we have a case of syphilis here in the cloister."

"Oh good," says Sister Catherine, "I was getting tired of that chablis."

The Cereal That Wasn't

During the 1992 Democratic Convention, *Spy* magazine published a widely distributed parody of the *New York Times* that included a version of the paper's (now defunct) "gossip column," which was called "Chronicle."

One of the items in that column reported that Cardinal John O'Connor was introducing Cardinal Crunch breakfast cereal. The bogus story described the product as a "low-sugar children's cereal made from nonconsecrated Eucharists or Holy Hosts," and quoted a Father David Stott, who was identified as from the New York archdiocese: "Church doctrine says the wafer cannot be used after it has been around for more than a year, so this seemed like as good a thing as any to do with leftovers. Also, it stays crunchy in milk."

The archdiocese was not amused. Communications Director Joseph Zwilling fired off a letter to the style editor of the *New York Times,* stating that there is no plan to market breakfast cereal, complaining that the author hadn't even bothered to check with the church, and demanding "a full correction and apology" from the *Times.*

—*From the* San Francisco Chronicle: *Personals by Leah Garchik*

23

ORIGINAL AND NOT SO ORIGINAL SINS

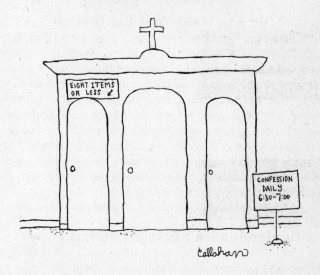

How do Catholics sin? Let me count the ways. There are sins against the Holy Spirit, mortal sins, near occasions of sin, sins of commission and omission, sins that cry to heaven for vengeance, venial sins, and original sin. No wonder we need so much time to examine our conscience.

A carpenter has a mad compulsion that he can't seem to control. Each day he steals lumber from his job site. The more he tries to control himself, the more difficult the problem becomes. Finally, the man goes to confession. "Father, forgive me, but I steal lumber. I don't mean to do it, but I just can't seem to help myself."

"I understand," says the priest. "For your penance, make a novena."

"Father," says the man, "I've never made one before, but if you have the plans, I have the lumber."

How to Make Your Confession

It is not only good manners but a duty for children to go to confession in the afternoon or at the time appointed for their confessions so as to leave the evenings for older persons who are not free to go at an earlier time. Every well-mannered child takes his turn going into the confessional; he never crowds, pushes, or goes too near the confessional; he does not talk, laugh, or giggle whilst waiting his turn to go, but carefully prepares for confession by examining his conscience and trying to be sorry for his sins. After confession, he does not rush out of the church, but remains to say his penance and thank God for once more pardoning him.

—*From* Manner and Good Manners *by Sister James Stanislaus*

Confession Isn't Easy for Priests Either

When I first started hearing confessions, I heard them all the time in the box. You have to listen so intently because you can't see the person. At the end of an hour I would be just exhausted. If there was a line I would come out and say, "I'll be back in a few minutes." At that time I was still smoking and I'd have a cigarette. Since you can't see the person you don't even know if they are male or female. When I was a young man and my voice hadn't changed yet, the priest told me, "Now be a good girl." I was just devastated; I felt awful. So you have to listen very carefully and ask questions. You have to consider how well educated the person is. The same advice is just not appropriate for everyone. It is a very intense experience. If I am doing a confession face-to-face and the person has been away for a while I will say, "Are you nervous?" and they usually say, "Yes." I say, "Well I'm not; it's going to be okay."

—*Anonymous Jesuit Priest*

Tim goes to confession and says to the priest, "Father, I have sinned. I am not married and I had sex with a woman six times last night."

"This is a terrible sin, my son. In order to forgive you I must have more details. Tell me, who was this woman? Was it Bridget O'Flahartey?"

"Oh no, Father, it wasn't Bridget."

"Was it Margaret Mary O'Malley?"

"No, Father, it wasn't Margaret Mary."

"Well then, was it Rosie O'Mara?"

"No, Father."

"I cannot forgive you unless you tell me her name," says the priest.

Tim is leaving the church and he runs into his friend Pete.

"So did the priest forgive you?" asks Pete.

"No," says Tim, "but I got a great list of names."

New and Exciting Ways to Sin

Deciding to tackle a procrastination problem, the Roman Catholic Church recently compiled its first worldwide addendum to the official list of sins since 1545, when the Council of Trent hammered out the acts and behaviors that put one's soul in jeopardy.

Here, according to the Rev. Francis Buckley, a Jesuit theology professor at the University of San Francisco, are some of the top new sins for the new year and beyond:

1) *Failing to vote*

2) *Drunken driving*

3) *Forging checks*

4) *Charging unjust rents*
5) *Paying unfair salaries*
6) *Wasting resources*
7) *Discrimination on the basis of sex, sexual orientation, age, religion, national origin, or handicap*
8) *Tax evasion*
9) *Doing shoddy work*
10) *Artificial manipulation of markets to inflate prices*
—Washington Post

Catch 22

The nuns told us to check the Ten Commandments to see if we had broken any of them. I got to adultery and I thought it was acting like an adult when you were a child. So at the age of seven, I confessed the sin of adultery. The priest told me it was a sin to confess a sin if you hadn't committed the sin. I was sinning while confessing my sins.

—*Brian Bouldrey, St. Mary's Star of the Sea parish,*
Jackson, Michigan

Thanks, Father, Now Everybody Knows

As a young man who had reached a certain age and discovered masturbation, I realized that I was going to have to tell about this in confession. I had to tell the priest that I "abused myself." I was in the confessional and I told the priest my great sin and he said, "How many times?" And I told him. In a very loud voice he said, "HOW MANY?" so that the entire church could hear him. When I came out of the confessional I was mortified; they all knew. And, of course, if you had to spend a long time saying your penance it was obvious to everyone how many times you had masturbated since your last confession.

—*John Gallagher, St. Matthew's parish,*
Cranston, Rhode Island

Each Saturday old Mrs. O'Malley goes to confession at Saint Patrick's church. Mrs. O'Malley is very deaf and when she is confessing her sins she has a tendency to shout. The priest suggests that she speak more quietly, since everyone in the church can hear what she is saying. Finally, the priest tells Mrs. O'Malley that it might be a good idea to write her sins down in advance.

The next Saturday Mrs. O'Malley kneels down in the confessional and hands the priest a piece of paper. The priest puts on his reading glasses and looks at the paper and says, "What's this? It looks like a grocery list."

"Oh my God!" shouts Mrs. O'Malley. "I must have left my sins in the A&P."

Beating the System

In order to avoid all the anxiety associated with going to confession we would go to the Italian parish, Saint Anthony's. The priests only spoke Italian and didn't understand (we hoped) what we were saying. No matter what sins you confessed (even if you had mugged your best friend's mother), they only gave you three Hail Mary's.

—*John Duff, St. Peter's parish, Troy, New York*

All Shook Up

In high school on Friday afternoons we'd have permission to leave class to go to confession. Most of us took advantage of this offer. A couple of guys who were really into the party circuit never went to confession. We all knew they were having a really good time. One of these guys was a great athlete but not very spiritual.

In San Francisco in 1957 we had a *really* good shaker of an earthquake. The students and the priest all darted under the desks. The athlete (who never went to confession) got up and said, "Father, I've got to go to confession." He ran out of the classroom and into the chapel.

—*Anonymous, St. Ignatius parish, San Francisco, California*

It's Worth the Wait

At our church we had two confessionals: one for Father Stevens and the other for Monsignor Manis. Father Stevens was a little deaf and couldn't really hear what you were saying. He always had the longer line. No one wanted to go to Monsignor Manis. He would say in the loudest voice possible, "You did what?" and he'd make you repeat your sin; then he would say it out loud, and I mean loud. "Why did you do that? How exactly did you do that?" On Saturday afternoons confessions were from two to four o'clock. You just wanted to get in and out as quickly as possible. The line for Father Stevens would be about twenty people and the line for Monsignor Manis would be nobody. Even though I had to wait forty-five minutes I always went to Father Stevens.

—*Rick Kelleher, Sacred Heart parish, East Grand Forks, Minnesota*

Honest, We Were Only Practicing

When I was making my first confession the nuns made us practice with sample sins. I went home and my mother was horrified at my terrible sins; she didn't get the concept of "practice" sins.

—*Richard Boyle, St. Adrian's parish, Chicago, Illinois*

It Just Doesn't Seem Fair

When they changed the laws about eating meat on Friday and it was no longer a mortal sin, I used to worry about the people in that transition week. Think about the people who ate a salami sandwich on that Friday before the church changed the rules and then died. They went to hell. The following week you could eat salami and you were home free. It just didn't seem fair. Even if you ate a salami sandwich when it was still a mortal sin, if you were alive at least you could get forgiveness. The injustice of it all.

—Marie Aranas, Sacred Heart parish, San Francisco, California

Watch Out for the Spin Cycle

Our Lord cleanses us as a washing machine cleans clothes so that our souls will be entirely clean.

—The New Saint Joseph Baltimore Catechism

A woman is in the confessional and she says, "Bless me Father for I have sinned. . . . I have not been to mass for months; I spend every Sunday morning on the golf course."

"God forgives you, my child. Is there anything else?"

"Yes, Father, I'm a hooker."

There is a long pause, then the priest says, "Don't worry about it. Just keep your head down and your left arm straight."

24

PATRON AND OTHER SAINTS

Catholics contemplate the exemplary life stories of the saints and invoke their comfort and aid. Many saints are noted for their patronage of specialized tasks (Saint Anthony—finder of lost articles; Saint Jude—hopeless causes), while other saints are the patrons of occupations (Saint Bartholomew—tanners; Saint Agatha—bell founders). But let's face it, how many of us today tan leather or work in a foundry? We need patron saints for today's world. Based on the information of the lives of saints found in the Oxford Dictionary of Saints, *the author offers recommendations for patron saints of the 1990s.*

The First Implants

Little is known of Saint Juthwara, but the story is, as a young girl she was very pious and spent a great deal of time praying and fasting. After the death of her beloved father she suffered from a great pain in her chest. Her wicked stepmother suggested that Saint Juthwara apply two cheeses to her chest to relieve the pain. Her equally wicked stepbrother (thinking the newly endowed saint was pregnant) killed Juthwara by striking off her head.

Saint Juthwara's unwitting chest enhancement deems her worthy to be named the patron of breast implants.

Unsafe Sex

Not much is recorded about the life of Saint Gwinear. We do know that he was a Welsh missionary who was martyred by Theodoric, king of Cornwall. There is one memorable miracle that is attributed to the saint. Two lovers were "caught in the act" on top of a bishop's tomb. The embarrassed lovers could not become disentangled until they were transported to Gwinear's tomb.

Gwinear's miraculous power to help this lovestruck (or stuck) couple makes him the perfect candidate to be the patron of unsafe sex.

The Flying Friar

Long before Sally Field donned a habit and became the "Flying Nun," there was Joseph of Copertino, the "Flying Friar." In the seventeenth century James joined the Franciscans and was ordained a priest. He became well known for his repeated levitations. On one occasion he helped workmen lift in midair a calvary cross 36 feet high. Ten men were unable to budge the cross but Joseph lifted it as if it were weightless. While he was in these states of ecstasy, burning, hitting, and pinpricks could not "awaken" him.

Look up in the sky—it's a bird, it's a plane, . . . no, it's Joseph of Copertino, the patron saint of superheroes who fight for truth, justice, and the Franciscan way.

Ashes to Ashes and Dust to Health Food

Saint Chad died in the seventh century. His first shrine was a wooden coffin shaped like a house with an opening on the side so the faithful could take out some of his dust. The saint's dust was mixed with water and used as a cure-all for men and cattle.

Saint Chad will be the patron of powdered health food mixes and vitamin supplements.

Early Labor Causes Big Pain

The English Saint Bettelin, it is alleged, was smitten with an Irish princess. He brought the very pregnant princess back to England. They were traveling in a forest when she went into heavy labor. Bettelin left her and went off to find a midwife. When he returned a pack of wild wolves was devouring the princess. Not surprisingly, after this grisly incident Bettelin became a hermit.

Saint Bettelin's tragedy could have been averted if only he had paid attention during that lecture, "What to Do If the Doctor Is Late!" Women whose labor pains are two minutes apart will beseech Saint Bettelin, the patron of Lamaze.

The Politically Correct Saint

Godric was a twelfth-century saint who lived the solitary life of a hermit. At first he survived on roots and berries; later he cultivated vegetables and built a wooden hut. In cold weather he would bring rabbits and field mice into his hut and warm them by the fire and then set them free. Once a deer was taking advantage of Godric's hospitality when the huntsman stopped by and asked the saint if he knew the whereabouts of the stag. Godric answered, "God knows where it is." The hunters apologized for disturbing Godric and rode off.

The saint's strict vegetarian diet and his fearless protection of an innocent deer—centuries before it would become politically correct—makes Godric the ideal candidate to be dubbed patron saint for animal rights activists.

The Hairy Saint

Wistan King of Mercia was martyred at the hand of his power-hungry cousin, who killed Wistan and three of his faithful followers. On the anniversary of his feast day each year on the spot where Wistan the martyr fell dead, his "hair" is said to grow from the ground.

No doubt, Saint Wistan's jealous cousin suffered from a nasty case of male-pattern baldness. From this day hence, Saint Wistan will be known as the patron of men who worship at the Hair Club for Men.

Did You Know There Was a Patron Saint of . . .

Cabdrivers and Hemorrhoids: Fiacre
Public Relations: Bernardine of Siena
Television: Clare of Assisi
Motorcyclists: Our Lady of Grace
Ecologists: Francis of Assisi
Hairdressers: Martin de Porres
Jurists: John Capistran
Happy Meetings: Raphael
Tax Collectors: Matthew
Travel Hostesses: Bona

In Case of Emergency Call on These Saints:

Saint Benedict: Poison sufferers
Saint Scholastica: Convulsive children
Saint Joseph: Dying
Saint Vitus: Epilepsy and motor diseases
Saint Catherine of Siena: Fire prevention
Saint Anne: Women in labor

Patron Saint of Realtors

As reported in the business section of *Time,* the slumping real estate market has proven a boon to religious gift shops. Hopeful home sellers are buying statues of Saint Joseph to be buried in their yards in the belief that the saint will help sell their house. The statue is buried head first and feet pointed heavenward. Custom dictates that once the house is sold, the Saint Joseph statue is exhumed and enshrined in the new home.

The head of the Catholic Information Center, Father James Coen, complained to the New York *Daily News* that real estate brokers "are turning this into a first-class sales gimmick." Heaven forbid!

25

RELIGIOUS RULES AND REGULATIONS

Part of the joy of being Catholic is the strict and unquestioning obedience to a welter of rules and regulations.

How to Sit

Sister Jambert told us girls to be sure to sit with our legs closed, especially while we wore our uniforms. She didn't want anyone "seeing into eternity."

—*Marcella Friel, St. Coleman's parish, Ardmore, Pennsylvania*

At his first Sunday mass the new priest gave a sermon against the Pill. After mass one of the parishioners shook his hand and said, "Father, if you don't play the game, don't make the rules."

Making the Right Impression

When you went to mass you HAD to go to communion. If you didn't, everyone in the church just assumed that you had committed a mortal sin. It was a peer pressure thing.

—*William Callahan, St. Aidan's parish, Jersey City, New Jersey*

Just What Would Happen?

We had to stand up when a priest came in the room or when the mother superior came in. We'd stand up and say,

"Good morning, Sister Mary Robert." Like something terrible would happen if you didn't.

—*Daniel Hernandez, Holy Family parish, San Antonio, Texas*

Isn't That How They Do It in Prison?

In high school we had three minutes to get to the next class. We had to walk single file, a foot apart from the person in front of us, and we couldn't speak. The priests and nuns worked the hallways making sure no one got out of line.

—*Coleen Martin, Our Lady of Lourdes parish, Decatur, Illinois*

Sign on the Dotted Line

In grammar school, my nun sent me home with a big plastic statue of the Blessed Virgin Mary. The bottom would unscrew and there would be a set of rosary beads. The idea was that the family would gather and say the rosary. We did it, because my parents had to sign a note that you brought back to the nun.

—*John Gallagher, Matthew's parish, Cranston, Rhode Island*

The Canon Law

When I was about ten years old, I was late for mass. There was a rule if you got in before the canon it was a venial sin and if you got in after the canon it was a mortal sin. I wasn't paying attention so I wasn't really sure if my sin was a venial sin or a mortal sin. Because I couldn't figure it out, the next time I went to confession I didn't say anything about it. That confession became a "bad" confession. I never did confess my sin of being late for mass, so all my subsequent confessions were "bad." I was living in a state of mortal sin and could have gone to hell at any moment.

—*Tony Byrne, St. Mary's Haddington Road parish, Dublin, Ireland*

Always in Groups of Five

Father Brown made us confess the sin of masturbation by saying "the sin of touch"—just "touch"; he didn't want any details. Father Fitzgibbons always wanted details. I used to go to confession every day because I would "touch" myself at night. It was a mortal sin, so I had to go to confession the very next day and pray that I wouldn't get killed overnight. I always confessed the sin of touch in groups of five: "Bless me Father for I have sinned. I touched myself five times." It was never a seven or a nine.

—*Michael Caulfield, Saint Eugene's parish, Chicago, Illinois*

A True Confession

I stole a package of Chicklets from the Grandway when I was eight. The next Saturday afternoon I went to confession. I told the priest that I had stolen the candy. He told me to say five Hail Mary's and five our Father's and make a "good" Act of Contrition. Not a "bad" Act of Contrition, a "good" one.

—*Linda Johnson, Blessed Sacrament parish, Waterbury, Connecticut*

26

THE ULTIMATE TEST OF FAITH

Today's Catholics face many tests of their faith: the high cost of parochial school tuition; the gluttonous urge to pig out on pork rinds and jelly donuts; and the temptation to watch lusty rock videos. But how do we really know how we measure up as Catholics? This multiple-choice quiz will determine how you rate as a soldier of Christ.

You have fifteen minutes to complete this test. Remember it's a sin to look at the quiz of the person sitting across the aisle from you.

1) There was something very unusual about the appearance of Saint Gwen Teirbron of Brittany. Was it
   A) At sixteen she was seven feet tall.
   B) Gwen was born a cyclops.
   C) Poor Gwen was completely bald.
   D) She had three breasts.

2) Indulgences we have gained can be
   A) Transferred to a close relative but only if that person is in the state of grace.
   B) Used as a guarantee that we won't die with mortal sin on our soul.
   C) Traded in for holy cards and rosary beads.
   D) Applied to the poor souls in purgatory.

3) Before he became pope, Paul III's nickname was "Cardinal Petticoat." Why?

    A) His sister was Pope Alexander VI's mistress.

    B) In his private chambers he would dress in a nun's habit.

    C) He was the first cardinal to wear those festive red robes.

    D) Before being ordained a priest he sold women's clothes and undergarments.

4) What was unusual about Senator Ted Kennedy's First Holy Communion?

    A) Ted, a precocious child, was only three years old.

    B) He was recouping from a tonsillectomy so the priest said mass in his hospital room.

    C) He received the sacrament in Vatican City from the pope himself.

    D) He choked on the communion wafer and almost died.

5) What is Simony?

    A) A game played at church bazaars similar to Bingo.

    B) The buying and selling of sacred offices.

    C) A form of fasting whereby the penitent only eats three-day-old fish.

    D) The study of church history.

6) What do we mean by a day of abstinence?

    A) A day on which we do not eat meat.

    B) We abstain from an activity that gives us pleasure and "offer up" our suffering.

    C) If we commit no sins on this day we are given a plenary indulgence.

    D) We refrain from performing unnecessary work.

7) Pope John Paul II
   A) Was shot in Saint Peter's Square while greeting tourists.
   B) Collects rare butterflies.
   C) Has an artificial knee.
   D) All of the above.

8) What is Septuagesima?
   A) An unconsecrated host.
   B) The two-week period before Lent.
   C) A formal name for the stations of the cross.
   D) Sinead O'Connor's confirmation name.

9) This Hollywood star once played Saint Francis of Assisi in a high school play.
   A) Robert DeNiro.
   B) Madonna.
   C) Kevin Costner.
   D) Danny DeVito.

10) Saint Blaise once healed a young boy who was choking to death on a fish bone. The blessing of Saint Blaise is administered on his feast day, February 3. The priest holds two candles at the throat of the person to be blessed. This traditional blessing is also given to
   A) Sick cattle.
   B) Fishermen about to go out to sea.
   C) Prisoners before they are hanged.
   D) Fish, dolphins, and whales.

11) In the book *My Six Popes* by French cardinal Jacques Martin, who scheduled the popes' audiences, he claims that
   A) Pope John XXIII scheduled his papal audiences in the afternoon because he liked to sleep late.

B) Pope John Paul II performed his first exorcism on a possessed woman who was visiting the Vatican.

C) Pope Pius XII was asked by Joe DiMaggio to throw out the first baseball during the 1949 World Series. The pope declined.

D) Pope John Paul I, before he died, had a papal visit scheduled with Fidel Castro.

12) This famous Catholic television personality was "roasted" at a Friar's Club by Jack Benny, Milton Berle, and Alan King.

A) Bishop Fulton Sheen.

B) Danny Thomas.

C) Ed Sullivan.

D) Lawrence Welk.

13) The martyred Saint Appollonia had all her teeth broken out from blows to her jaw. Is she remembered

A) As the patron saint of prizefighters.

B) With a dental publication named *Appollonian*.

C) By a prayer named for her that is dedicated to plastic surgeons.

D) With a statue of her holding a flower in one hand and her teeth in the other.

14) Who is Chuck White?

A) The first Catholic to be elected a U.S. senator in 1824.

B) A young boy from New Jersey who was cured of acne by Mother Teresa.

C) A sixteenth-century Jesuit priest who was martyred by being pelted to death with hot cross buns.

D) A serialized comic hero featured in the Catholic publication *Treasure Chest*.

15) Pope Clement II was the only pope
   A) To have a career as a professional boccie ball player.
   B) Who was allergic to the smoke from burning candlewax.
   C) Buried in Germany.
   D) To be accused of bigamy.

16) When the Black Death swept through Europe it is estimated that it killed about one-third of the population. What percentage of the clergy succumbed?
   A) Miraculously, only 10 percent.
   B) 40 percent.
   C) An astonishing 90 percent of the clergy died. The plague almost ended religious life as we know it.
   D) No one knows for sure. The Vatican forbade the religious orders to release the information.

17) A nun killed her mother with a crucifix after seeing this film.
   A) *The Ten Commandants.*
   B) *The Exorcist.*
   C) *Sister Act.*
   D) *The Rosary Murders.*

18) When were Catholic priests first banned from having wives?
   A) It is not an official policy. It is a tradition dating from the time of Christ's life on earth.
   B) The first local legislation on the matter dates back to 306 in Elvira, Spain.
   C) In 1227 when Pope Benedict XII gave up his wife and family when he was elected pontiff.
   D) The year was 1136. Cardinal Bono—who was trapped in an unhappy marriage—was not granted an annulment by the Holy See.

19) The television series "The Flying Nun," which aired from 1967 to 1970, was condemned by some religious orders because

    A) None of the show's profits were donated to the nuns.

    B) The show's star, Sally Field, was not a Catholic.

    C) In one episode the Flying Nun was referred to as "de plane, de plane."

    D) The show "humanized" nuns and their work.

20) Emperor Leo III the Isaurian launched a campaign against

    A) Iconoclasm, the veneration of sacred images and relics.

    B) The use of costly incense burned during church services.

    C) Too many fast days in the liturgical calendar.

    D) That "devil-influenced" printing press used to produce the bible.

21) After saying a decade of Hail Mary's on our rosary beads we ponder one of the mysteries. The Five Glorious Mysteries are (1) the Resurrection, (2) the Ascension, (3) the descent of the Holy Spirit, (4) the Assumption, and (5)

    A) The Annunciation.

    B) The Apparition.

    C) The Coronation.

    D) The Vaccination.

22) Father Andrew Greeley, author of such popular works of fiction as *The Cardinal Sins* and *Thy Brother's Wife*,

    A) Has been excommunicated from the Catholic Church.

    B) Gave away the first million dollars he made.

    C) Claims he has a "ghost writer"—the Holy Spirit.

    D) Won the Nobel Prize for Literature in 1974.

23) By decree of the *Sixth Provincial Council of Baltimore* in 1846, who is the patron of the United States of America?
  A) Christopher the ex-saint.
  B) The Blessed Virgin Mary.
  C) Saint John of the Fruited Plain.
  D) Mother Cabrini.

24) A game made in France called *Catechic* is a religious trivia game. The game is special because
  A) It was blessed by Pope John Paul II.
  B) It's easy to win if you play against non-Catholics.
  C) Merv Griffin is producing a television quiz show based on the game.
  D) The game is sold only at Vatican City, with the profits going to the Society for the Propagation of the Faith.

25) The seven gifts of the Holy Ghost are wisdom, understanding, counsel, fortitude, knowledge, piety, and
  A) Exorcism.
  B) Fear of the Lord.
  C) A free pair of Easy Spirit walking shoes.
  D) Faith.

What's Your Rating as a Catholic?

(Answers: 1-D, 2-D, 3-A, 4-C, 5-B, 6-A, 7-A, 8-B, 9-D, 10-A, 11-B, 12-A, 13-B, 14-D, 15-C, 16-B, 17-B, 18-B, 19-D, 20-A, 21-C, 22-B, 23-B, 24-A, 25-B.)

  20–25 Possible candidate for canonization
  15–20 Pious
  10–15 Not a great Catholic but a good one
  5–10 Obviously nonpracticing
  0–5 Heathen

27

IN CASE OF ACCIDENT, CALL A PRIEST

The Catholic Way of Death

Catholics are fortunate to have an "extra edge" when it comes to winning everlasting salvation. When the end is near, we are given one last chance to make things right with our Maker. Maybe that's the reason there are so many Catholics in heaven.

Hennessey is at the racetrack when he spots Father Ryan making the sign of the cross over one of the horses. He takes

this as a sign from God and bets all his money on the horse. The horse finishes last.

Hennessey finds Father Ryan and says, "Father, I saw you blessing that horse, so I put all my money on him."

"I wasn't blessing him," says the priest. "I was administering the last rites."

Something They Forgot to Teach Us in the Seminary

One time I got a phone call and the person asked if I knew what prayers to say to raise the dead. I just thought it was your basic crazy person so I gave the guy the name and number of a priest friend who needed an exciting phone call. I said, "Call him and ask your question."

—*Anonymous Jesuit Priest*

Fred's old basset hound Pepper died. Fred had had Pepper since he was a pup, and the two had been inseparable. Fred was brokenhearted and decided to give his old pal a fitting send-off. Fred went to the Lutheran church and asked the pastor if he would give Pepper a proper funeral service in his church. The pastor replied, "In our faith we believe that dogs have no soul. It would be improper to perform such a ceremony."

Next, Fred called a rabbi and asked him if he would consent to holding a service for Pepper. The rabbi said, "I understand the great love you have for your pet, but in our religion dogs are ritually unclean. It would be impossible for me to fulfill your request."

Finally, he knocked on the door of the local Catholic church. Father Cassidy listened to Fred's request and said, "At least once a week we have someone stopping by the rectory with a story just like yours. As much as I sympathize with your situation, it is strictly forbidden by Holy Mother Church to do such a thing."

"I am very sorry to hear that, Father," said Fred. "To show you how much a proper burial means to me, I was prepared to donate $10,000 to any church that would give my Pepper a religious send-off."

Father Cassidy paused for a moment, then said, "Let me see if I understand all the facts of the situation. You say Pepper was a Catholic dog?"

Frank, a wealthy executive, is dying. His business partner Joe is in the room when the priest arrives to administer the last rites. Joe and the priest talk for a few minutes, then it's time to give Frank the last rites. Frank makes his last confession. He tells the priest, "Father, I stole a million dollars from my business partner Joe. He never knew that it was me who took his boat out on the lake and sank it. I was a terrible friend. I had an affair with Joe's wife. Father, do you think Joe will forgive me for these terrible sins?"

The priest says, "Don't worry about it. Joe just told me he poisoned you."

Going to a Good Cause

When my husband died people gave me money for masses and what have you. I gave the money to the nuns. One day they called me and said, "Want to come and see what we bought with your money?" The nuns had each bought a La-Z-Boy recliner. It was all right because they prayed for my husband.

—*Marie Good, Our Lady of the Ridge parish, Chicago Ridge, Illinois*

Two farmers chip in and buy an animal to work the land. Frank says they have a mule and Mike insists that it is a donkey. They decide to let the parish priest settle the dispute. Father Smith says, "According to the bible, what you have is an ass."

The men go back to their farms and discover that the animal is dead. They are digging a grave when Father Smith walks by and says, "Are you guys digging a posthole?"

Frank and Mike look up and say, "Not according to the bible!"

A bus filled with the ladies from the Altar and Rosary Society is returning from a church picnic. There is a terrible accident and everyone in the bus is killed. They get to the Pearly Gates, where Saint Peter tells them that the new addition to heaven is not yet complete. They will have to wait in hell until the construction work is finished.

Two weeks later and Saint Peter gets a call from Satan: "Pete, you gotta get these women outta here."

Saint Peter says, "I can't. The extra room isn't ready. I have nowhere to put them."

"You gotta do something," says the devil. "With their bake sales and rummage sales they are only fifty dollars short of air-conditioning this place."

Just Your Typical Italian Funeral

At a typical Italian funeral, usually there was a grieving widow dressed all in black. The widow would be carrying on a normal conversation and all of a sudden it was time to wail. "Oh what will I do without him? . . . " That was the cue for all the other women of her age group to chime in; it would become an Italian chorus of crying and wailing women. The tradition was for the widow to hurl herself toward the coffin; two of the male members of the family would hold her back. One time my mother was attending one of these operatic-type wakes at the tender age of nine. When it came time for the traditional "widow hurl" the woman actually broke free of the men and fell on top of the casket. The bier came falling down and the body fell out of the coffin and rolled toward my school-age mother. To this day my mother has to be physically dragged to wakes.

—William Callahan, St. Aidan's parish, Jersey City, New Jersey

The bell ringer in the local parish dies, so the priest puts an ad in the newspaper for a replacement. The next day there is a terrible noise at the door. The pastor opens the door and there stands a man who has no arms. The armless man says, "I've come about the job." The priest says, "My good man, how could you possibly ring the bell?" "I'll show you," answers the man. Before the priest can stop him, the man hurries to the bell tower. He positions himself in front of the bell and counts to ten. Then he aims his head at the bell and runs into it with all his force. There is a great GONG! The bell swings back and hits the bell ringer and he falls out of the tower onto the concrete sidewalk below. The pastor rushes to his side to administer last rites. A concerned bystander says to the pastor, "Father, who is that man?"

A few days later, there is a terrible noise at the pastor's door. He opens it and discovers another man with no arms who claims to be the twin of the deceased bell ringer. He asks for the job as the bell ringer. When the pastor objects, the man begs the pastor to let him try out for the position. The man scurries up to the bell tower, puts his head down, and runs at the bell. This time the bell ringer misses the bell and falls out of the tower and lands on the sidewalk. The pastor rushes down to give him last rites. A bystander says to the pastor, "Who is that man?"

The priest says, "I don't know, but he's a dead ringer for the other guy."

Just Hanging Around

The nun wanted us to know how much Jesus had suffered on Good Friday on the cross. She made all of us stand up and stretch out our arms and just stand there—it seemed like forever. I was thinking, "Poor Jesus, poor Jesus, I'd never want to be hung on a cross."

—*Shirley Kowal, St. Margaret's parish, Chicago, Illinois*

Paul and Father Brown are playing golf at the local country club. Paul is having a terrible time hitting the ball and when he does it lands in the rough. Each time he swings at the ball he says, "Oh shit!"

After many "Oh shit's!" the priest says, "You have to watch your language or God will punish you."

But a few minutes later Paul drives his ball into the sand trap and yells, "Oh shit!"

A hand reaches out of a huge cloud and it thrusts down a huge bolt of lightning, which hits Father Brown. A deep voice comes out of the cloud and says, "Oh shit!"

One Way to Make Converts

On my Uncle Archie's deathbed, the very night he died, my aunt had him converted to Catholicism. Uncle Archie was unconscious at the time! My aunt thought the only way he'd go to heaven was if he was a Catholic like she was. The whole family was in an uproar. How dare she make him a Catholic when he's unconscious and dying.

—*Diane Conway, Methodist, Charleston, South Carolina*

The End

At the end of one mass, the priest turned around and said, "Go in peace. The world has ended." The entire congregation responded, "Thanks be to God."

—*Anonymous Jesuit Priest*